Black Thursday, Blue Monday

In Search of the Curse of the Washington Nationals

A Baseball Whodunit

Black Thursday, Blue Monday

In Search of the Curse of the Washington Nationals

A BASEBALL WHODUNIT

David Bledsoe

Copyright © 2019 David Bledsoe

All rights reserved.

ISBN-13: 9781093400953
ISBN-10: 1093400951

CHAPTER 1

Black Thursday

It was Thursday, October 12, 2017. It was the top of the fifth inning in Game 5, and when Dusty Baker handed the ball to Max Scherzer, it was finally going to happen. The Washington Nationals were about to do something they had never done. They were going to achieve their first playoff series win, and advance to the National League Championship Series.

Since 2012, the Nationals had been one of the best teams in baseball – during the regular season. In those six seasons, the Nats had won 555 regular season games, more than any other team in baseball with the sole exception of the Los Angeles Dodgers. They had led all of baseball with 98 wins in 2012, and led the National League in 2014 with 96. Yet they had never won a single playoff series. Not one. In 2012, a first round loss to the Cardinals. In 2014, a first round loss to the Giants. And in 2016, a first round loss to the Dodgers. All with home field advantage.

When the team, previously the Montreal Expos, moved to Washington in 2005, it had continued the Expos' perennial role as the doormat of the league, finishing dead last in its division for five of its first six years in D.C. But the vibe had started to change in 2010. After losing 102 games in 2008, the Nationals had acquired the No. 1 draft pick in all of baseball. They used it to select Stephen Strasburg, a flamethrowing pitcher from San Diego State, and by midseason 2010 had stuck him into their starting rotation as their ace. After losing 103 games in 2009, the Nats again had the No. 1 draft pick in 2010, and drafted a player whom teams had been salivating over ever since he made the cover of Sports Illustrated as a 16-year-old: Bryce Harper.

In spring training in 2012, with Harper finally expected to join the big club, baseball writers far and wide proclaimed the Nationals as the up-and-coming National League power. And, when Harper was called up in mid-April, the Nats, as predicted, took off. On May 22, they claimed first place in the National League East for good. They went on to win 98 games, the most in the National League.

But despite home field advantage, they lost their first playoff series in Game 5 to the St. Louis Cardinals in heartbreaking fashion. In 2013, after being declared the preseason favorite to win the NL pennant, if not the World Series, they suffered a late season collapse and watched the hated Braves take the division. The next year, 2014, the Nationals righted the ship, running away with the division with 96 wins, only to again lose the NLDS, this time to the San Francisco Giants in four games.

So, despite all their regular season success, the Nationals' postseasons had been nothing but futility. In 2015, the Nats' owners, the Lerner family, had had enough. They went out and signed the top free agent available, the man that would take them to the Promised Land. Max Scherzer.

Scherzer had won a Cy Young with the Detroit Tigers in 2013 and just come off an 18-5 year with 252 strikeouts. Scherzer would not come cheap. The Tigers had tried to re-sign him with an annual $24 million salary, which would have made him one of the six best-paid players in the game. He turned it down. The previously penurious Nats topped that offer, giving Scherzer a seven year contract worth $30 million a year with a $50 million signing bonus, a record at the time. They had their man. There would be no more first round exits from the playoffs for Washington.

The baseball press doubled down. There was no way that this ridiculously loaded team could not be the World Series favorites. But despite the addition of Scherzer, the Nats imploded in 2015. Beset by injuries, the team finished seven games behind the Mets and barely escaped a sub-.500 season. It was "wait 'til next year" once more.

But in 2016, the Nationals were finally ready to prove the pundits right. They wreaked havoc on the rest of the NL East, winning 94 games and home field advantage for the first-round NLDS against the Dodgers.

In that series, after the teams split the first two games, the Nationals won Game 3 at Los Angeles. That meant they only had to win one of the next two games to advance to the NL Championship. After losing Game 4 to the Dodgers in a one-run game, the Nationals turned to the $30 million man, Max Scherzer, to bring them home in Game 5. Disaster struck again. When the Nats bullpen coughed up the lead, the Dodgers called in their closer, Kenley Jansen, two innings early, in the seventh, to face the Nats. When Jansen ran out of gas in the ninth, they brought in none other than Clayton Kershaw, the Dodgers' ace and at this point the best pitcher in baseball. Despite the fact that he had just pitched 6 2/3 innings in the previous game, Kershaw recorded the last two outs – his first and likely last save as a major leaguer-- and the Nats had once again snatched defeat from the jaws of victory.

Now, here, a year later, on October 12, 2017, the tables had turned. The Nationals were now facing the Cubs in the fifth and deciding game of the 2017 National League Division Series, and now they were about to do exactly to the Cubs what the Dodgers had done to them. This was the situation that the Nationals and their fans had openly, passionately prayed for. Max Scherzer, the best pitcher in the league, was going to the mound to close out Game 5.

Scherzer is a bulldog of a pitcher, one of the most competitive athletes in the game. After one of his myriad strikeouts, he stalks around the mound, impatient for the ball to be returned to him by his third baseman, champing at the bit to deal the same fate to the next batter. If a manager comes to the mound in the middle of a game to take the ball from Scherzer's hand, he better be ready for a fight. Max has been known to disagree, vociferously, with such decisions, and he has sent more than one manager back to the bench, empty-handed, to reflect on the folly of his suggestion. He's also one of the most cerebral strategists in the pitching fraternity, making adjustments batter by batter, depending on what is working for him that night. If his fastball, which tops out at 97-98 mph, isn't working, he will happily rely on his frisbee slider, or his equally effective curve, or drop a late-breaking changeup on a hapless batter.

The ultimate pitching accomplishment is the perfect game, which has only been accomplished 23 times in MLB history. Well, in 2015, Scherzer nearly pitched two perfect games: he lost one with two outs in the ninth inning on a very questionable hit-by-pitch, and the other because his third baseman kicked a groundball in the sixth. Each time, he had to settle for a mere no-hitter instead.

Scherzer's 2016 was equally spectacular. He had won the 2016 National League Cy Young, leading the league in wins (20), games started (34), innings pitched (228), strikeouts (284), and WHIP[1] (0.968). On May 11, 2016, against his former Tigers teammates, Scherzer recorded 20 strikeouts in a game, tying the MLB record held by Roger Clemens, Randy Johnson, and Kerry Wood. On June 11 of that year, he notched his 2000th career strikeout, the third-fastest pitcher to reach that mark, behind only Nolan Ryan and the aforementioned Kershaw.

When he took the mound in Game 5 of the division series against the Cubs, Scherzer was on his way to winning the 2017 Cy Young as well, again leading the league with 268 strikeouts and a ridiculous WHIP of 0.902. (He would garner 27 out of 30 votes as the best pitcher in the league.) He had even pitched an "immaculate inning" against the Philadelphia Phillies in May, throwing just nine pitches to strike out the side. In June, he flirted with what would have been his third career no-hitter only to lose the bid in the eighth inning. There was no debate. Mad Max was the man that the Nats wanted with the ball.

---

1. Walks and hits per inning, a stat invented by baseball writer Daniel Okrent, and thought by many to be the ultimate criterion to judge a pitcher's skill. Scherzer's 2017 WHIP was the 15th lowest recorded by a starter since World War II.

Scherzer had missed the first two games of the NLDS due to a hamstring cramp suffered in the last week of the regular season. But he started Game 3 in Chicago, and he left no doubt that he was back, no-hitting the Cubs' powerful lineup for six innings. Up 1-0, he left the game in the seventh after surrendering his first hit to Ben Zobrist. But Scherzer's brilliant day was for naught: the Nats' bullpen allowed Zobrist to score on a single by Albert Almora, and then gave up another in the eighth to lose, 2-1.

But now, in the winner-take-all Game 5, the Nationals' shaky bullpen was not going to be allowed to blow another game. A four-run second inning staked the Nats to a 4-1 lead, but when Nats starter Gio Gonzalez gave up two more runs in the top of the third, Max Scherzer headed to the bullpen to warm up. The place went wild.

As Scherzer took the mound in the top of the fifth to protect the one-run lead, the Nationals fans leapt to their feet and roared their unanimous approval of manager Dusty Baker's move. On two days' rest, Scherzer was in to apply the *coup de grace* in front of the packed house. There was no doubt about it. The best pitcher in the league, the gamer, was in, and he was going to pitch until his arm fell off. The Cubs were toast.

The first batter to face Scherzer for the Cubs was Kris Bryant – the 2016 Most Valuable Player in the National League, as well as the Rookie of the Year in 2015. On three pitches, Scherzer induced a groundout to short. Next up, the slugging Anthony Rizzo saw another three pitches and flew out to center. Two outs, six pitches. Max was cruising. Nationals Park was in ecstasy.

What happened next was a meltdown unprecedented in the entire history of the game of professional baseball.

First, Wilson Contreras hit a bouncer up the middle. Shortstop Trea Turner raced into the shallow outfield grass, gloved it and came up throwing, but Contreras, hustling down the line, beat it out for an infield hit. Next, Ben Zobrist, pinch-hitting, hit a seeing-eye popup to left that dropped in no-man's land for a single. First and second, two outs. Not to worry. Max needed only to punch out Addison Russell, the Cubs shortstop, just like he had 272 other batters that year.

But Russell ripped a double down the third base line past the diving Anthony Rendon, scoring both runners. And the Cubs had taken the lead, 5-4. Scherzer's shoulders slumped.

The next Cubs batter, Jason Heyward, was still grinding through a year-long slump, but with first base open, the Nats decided to walk him intentionally to pitch to the right-handed Javier Baez. Working from the stretch, Scherzer threw a pitch. Strike one. He threw a second pitch. Strike two. If he threw a third, the inning was over, and the Nats would have four more at-bats to score two runs to win the game.

Scherzer drew himself up, checked the runner at second, and threw a beautiful slider that dropped off the table. Baez swung wildly, and missed it by a foot. Strike three.

Except the slider passed under the glove of the Nats' catcher, Matt Wieters. A dropped third strike. The ball rolled to the backstop. Baez hesitated, then took off for first. Wieters, momentarily distracted when Baez's bat brushed his head on the follow-through, raced after the ball. He corralled it, wheeled and fired to get the out at first. But his throw sailed well to the right of first baseman Ryan Zimmerman and into right field. By the time the Nats had collected the ball, Russell had scored, Heyward was on third, and Baez was at second. 6-4, Cubs.

The fiasco wasn't over. Pinch hitter Tommy La Stella, up next, swung on a 1-1 fastball from Scherzer. His swing nicked Matt Wieters's glove, and the umpire correctly awarded La Stella first base on catcher's interference. Bases loaded, (still) two outs.

Scherzer looked wildly about, like a man who had lost his mind. Still, there was no one coming to get him. This was the moment that he, and every Nats fan, had asked for. Him, on the mound, with the game on the line.

The next Cubs batter, Jon Jay, stepped in. Scherzer threw a ball, outside. His next pitch, a foul ball.

Then, the only thing that had not yet happened in this farcical inning happened. Scherzer overthrew a cut fastball, which sailed and drilled Jay on his back leg. Jay took first on a hit-by-pitch, and all the runners advanced. Heyward trotted home to add a seventh run to the Cubs' tally: 7-4.

Batting next was Kris Bryant. That meant that the Cubs had batted around in the inning against the best pitcher in the league. When Scherzer retired Bryant on a popup to short, he had thrown 28 pitches, and had surrendered three hits and four runs. To put this in perspective, in 32 starts that year, Scherzer had only allowed an opposing team to score four runs in five of those games. Here, he allowed four runs in a single inning. The Inning From Hell.

There is a well-known baseball trivia question which goes: "Name the four ways for a batter to get to first base without even hitting the baseball." The answers are: a walk; to be hit by a pitch; reach on a dropped third strike; and catcher's interference.

All of those happened in Max's Meltdown inning. Consecutively.

Heyward: walk. Baez: dropped third strike. La Stella: catcher's interference. Jay: hit by pitch.

Catcher's interference, for the love of God! A major league baseball season consists of approximately 2,430 separate games. In most seasons, there are fewer than two dozen instances of catcher's interference in all of those 2,430 games. Given roughly 180,000 total plate appearances by batters in a baseball season, the chance of reaching first on catcher's interference is roughly 0.0002 – or two one-hundredths of a percent.

In a nine-season career, Wieters had caught in 930 games and over 8,000 innings, for 34,221 batters. He had been called for five catcher's interferences in his career, or one every 6,844 batters. He had none in 2017 until the fateful night. [2]

Baseball is a game of well-kept records. To understand the magnitude of the disaster of Scherzer's inning, consider this. In the history of professional baseball, going back almost to the Civil War, there have been roughly 225,000 games. The good folks at Baseball-Reference have a database of records for about 70% of those – about 2.75 million

---

2. Scherzer had faced 7719 batters in his career. He had hit 66, less than one percent.

half-innings. There is no record of any half-inning in which all five events occurred: a hit, a runner reaching by a dropped third strike, an intentional walk, a catcher's interference, and a hit-batsman. Not once, in nearly three million half-innings of recorded games, had Max's Inning from Hell ever occurred.

If the game had ended at that point, it would be safe to say that the Nationals were cursed. What Nats fans had just witnessed was the baseball equivalent of the *Hindenberg*, the *Titanic*, and the Battle of Little Big Horn all rolled up together. But those fans were in for even more torture. In the top of the sixth, with one on and two outs, the Nats' left fielder Jayson Werth would misjudge a routine line drive, allowing it to drop in for a "double." The runner scored, increasing the Cubs lead to 8-4.

For Washington fans, the game was over. Or was it? Could the Nationals find a way, even after the Inning from Hell, find a way to claw their way back into this game?

True torture comes from the Greek myth of Tantalus. For his crimes of killing his son Pelops and serving him as an entrée to the Olympian gods, Tantalus was sentenced by Rhadamanthus, Aeacus, and Minos, the three judges of the Greek afterlife, to a peculiar eternal punishment. Tantalus was doomed to be perpetually hungry and thirsty, while standing in a pool of water and under a fruit tree bristling with ripe, delicious fruit. Whenever Tantalus stooped to quench his thirst from the pool around his knees, the water would instantly seep away into the ground. Whenever he reached to pluck an apple off the tree, the branches would suddenly recede up out of his reach. Hence, the word "tantalize" – to torment by making something appear attainable, then pulling it away.

Yes, the fans of the Nationals had even more to endure. The Nats would, even after Max's debacle, rally to dangle an improbable apple of a win over their victory-starved fans, only to snatch it away once again.

In the bottom of the sixth, with the Nats down 8-4, Jayson Werth walked, and Bryce Harper doubled. The Cubs pitcher wild-pitched Werth home. 8-5, Cubs. Zimmerman then walked, and Daniel Murphy followed with a double to the wall, plating Harper. 8-6, Cubs, with three innings left to play.

Both teams added a single run in the 7th, to make the score 9-7. The clock struck midnight as the teams went on to the eighth. Now Friday morning, Murphy led off the bottom of the eighth for Washington with a walk, and Rendon followed with another walk. Adam Lind, representing the winning run, came to the plate as a pinch hitter. Lind had had a phenomenal year as a pinch-hitter for the Nats, crushing four home runs in his first 47 pinch hit at-bats. The stadium, rising from the ashes like a phoenix, again erupted. It was going to happen. Another apple dangled – despite all the disasters that had occurred, the Nats were going to win this game.

But it was not to be this time, as Lind grounded into a 4-6-3 double play. The fans groaned and again fell back in their seats in silence.

But Murphy had advanced to third on the play. With two outs, there was yet more Tantalus to come. Michael Taylor, who had been on fire all series, drove a single up the middle, and Murphy trotted home to bring the Nats to within a single run, 9-8. The next batter was catcher Jose Lobaton. Lobaton, batting only .170 that year, was facing Wade Davis, the Cubs closer, who had recorded 32 saves that year. With two outs, it didn't look good.

But to the wonderment of all, including probably himself, Lobaton laced a single to center, and the place went nuts. Now, it was the Cubs fans' turn to be glum. The Nationals had the tying and winning runs on base. On second, the speedy Taylor would score on any ball that got out of the infield, and the Nats had the top of the lineup coming up.

The Cubs catcher, Wilson Contreras, has a tricky habit – he loves to throw to first base to pick off napping runners. Lobaton and all the Nats knew this was Contreras' special play. Moreover, it made no sense for Lobaton to get an extra lead from first – second base was occupied by Taylor. There was nowhere to go. And despite all that, Jose Lobaton wandered too far off first base. Contreras noticed, as did first baseman Anthony Rizzo. As Contreras caught Davis's fastball, Rizzo darted behind Lobaton, and Contreras rifled it to Rizzo, who dropped a quick tag on Lobaton. The umpire signaled safe. A close call, but still alive.

But the Cubs appealed the decision to the video-watching umpire in New York. Two of the umpires went over to the equipment and put on the headphones that allowed them to hear the decision of the New York office. With the entire stadium hardly daring to breath, the crew chief, Jerry Layne, took off his headphones and gave the out signal. Lobaton was out, and the inning was over.

As was the game. The Nationals went down in order in the ninth against Wade Davis. Turner, flyout. Werth, strikeout. Bryce Harper, the Nats' golden boy, the NL MVP in 2015, could tie the game with a single stroke. He struck out on a full count. It was now almost 2:00 AM Friday morning, and the Nats were once again cleaning out their lockers after their first playoff series.

It was the single most bizarre game with the single most bizarre Inning from Hell that had ever been played in major league history. Tim Kurkjian, ESPN senior baseball writer, called it "the best and stupidest game I've ever seen in my entire life."

The knife had a final twist to come, two weeks later. During the World Series, MLB's chief baseball officer Joe Torre confirmed that the umpiring crew working the game made the wrong call in Max's disastrous inning. On the dropped third strike to Baez, Baez's follow-through swing grazed Wieters' mask, and under MLB rules, the passed ball became a dead ball. Since it was strike three, Baez should have been called out. It would have been the third out of the inning. Scherzer would have left the inning having given up no runs, and the Nats still holding a 5-4 lead.

The things that had to go wrong for the Nats for them to lose this game are almost too many to count.

There can be only one answer. When mathematical probability has no answer, we must turn to superstition. Yes, the Nationals are definitely, positively, to an absolute metaphysical certainty, a cursed baseball team.

Disbelievers can scoff all they like. But an examination of the details of the Nationals' playoff history renders all other theories untenable.

In fact, as we examine the twists and turns of the Nationals' past, it becomes clear that Max's Inning from Hell was merely the exclamation point – a spectacular one, no doubt – on the Curse of the Nationals.

But *why* are the Washington Nationals under a curse? To determine that, we are first going to need to explore the history of baseball curses. Perhaps once we have an understanding of other teams' curses, and the various origins of those curses, then we can apply that knowledge and follow the clues to discover the source of the Nationals' Curse.

CHAPTER 2

The Curses: How the Outcome of Baseball Games is Determined By Broadway Shows, Barnyard Animals, and/or, Sometimes, Kentucky Fried Chicken

TO PARAPHRASE A ONCE-POPULAR SELF-HELP book, why do bad things happen to good teams?

Take the Boston Red Sox. Founded in 1901 as the Boston Americans, they won the World Series in their third year of existence. They won it again in 1912, 1915, 1916, and 1918. And then, almost a century of misery followed.

After that 1918 Series, the Red Sox didn't return to the Series again until almost thirty years later, in 1946. Featuring Hall of Famer Ted Williams, they won 104 games that year, but would lose the World Series to the Cardinals that year, by a single run in Game 7 on one of the most famous plays in Series history, Enos Slaughter's "Mad Dash." In the eighth inning of Game 7, Cardinals right fielder Slaughter scored from first base on a bloop single to centerfield.[3]

Twenty years passed without another pennant for the Sox. Then, in 1967, paced by Carl Yazstremski's Triple Crown year (leading the league in batting average, home runs, and RBI), the Red Sox won the pennant,

---

3. The play was officially scored a double, but was in truth only a single. Red Sox second baseman Johnny Pesky was hesitant on the throw home, and the batter, Harry "The Hat" Walker, merely advanced to second on Pesky's late throw.

and faced the St. Louis Cardinals again. Down three games to one, the Red Sox's chances looked bleak. But they came roaring back to win Game 5, then Game 6 to tie the Series at 3 games apiece. And again, as in 1946, they would lose Game 7.

Eight years later, it's 1975, and the Bosox won the pennant again. They would face Cincinnati's powerful Big Red Machine, stocked with stars like Pete Rose, Johnny Bench, and Joe Morgan. Cincinnati took three of the first five games. With Boston facing elimination in Game 6, the Reds took a 6-3 lead. But the Bosox improbably scored three runs in the eighth to tie the game, which then went to extra innings. In the bottom of the 12th, Red Sox catcher Carlton Fisk hit one of the most memorable home runs in baseball history – down the left field line, as Fisk danced down the line to first, waving the ball fair, *willing* the ball fair, to win the game and send it to Game 7. Which the Red Sox then lost. By a single run. In the ninth inning.

Three years later, the Red Sox were up seven games on the last day of August, but end up tied with the dastardly Yankees at the end of the regular season. There will have to be a one-game playoff. At Fenway, the Sox went out to a 2-0 lead, only to watch the Yankees' light-hitting shortstop, Bucky Dent, hit a towering home run over the Green Monster in left field. Yankees win, 5-4. For his feat, Red Sox fans have given Dent an added honorary Anglo-Saxon middle name, a name by which he is still known in Boston: "Bucky @#$%^&* Dent."

In 1986, the Sox, loaded with Roger Clemens, Oil Can Boyd, Dwight Evans, Jim Rice, and Wade Boggs, took the AL championship and faced the Mets in the Series. After five games, Boston led, 3 games to 2. In Game 6, tied after nine innings, in the 10th, Dave Henderson hit a leadoff home run for the Red Sox, and the Sox tacked on another to lead 5-3. The Red Sox needed to record three outs to win their first World Series since Woodrow Wilson was president.

All year, whenever the Red Sox had a lead in the last inning, manager McNamara has made the same move. The Red Sox's first baseman, Bill Buckner, was a hitter par excellence, but years of leg injuries severely hampered his mobility. So routinely, with a late inning lead, McNamara would lift Buckner for Dave Stapleton, a mediocre hitter but a much better fielder. But here, three outs away from the world championship, McNamara decided he wanted to reward Buckner, a 17-year veteran who had never been on a World Series winner, and let him be on the field for the inevitable celebration. Buckner stayed in the game.

Every baseball fan knows what happened next. Wally Backman flied out. Keith Hernandez flied out. One more out would end seven decades of Bosox frustration. But Gary Carter singled, as did the next batter, Kevin Mitchell. Ray Knight singled to the gap in right, and Carter scored. The Red Sox lead was cut to a single run.

But they still only needed a single out.

The Red Sox brought in their closer, Bob Stanley. Stanley promptly uncorked a wild pitch, allowing Mitchell to score from third, tying the game.

At this point, the Sox are deflated, but hope is still in the air. The game is tied – they can still win if they get out of the inning. Stanley wound up and fired to the Mets' next batter, Mookie Wilson. He tapped a slow roller to first base – finally, the third out the Bosox need to get out of the inning. Buckner ranged to field the ball, which he would flip to Stanley, covering, for the third out. And the ball rolled under his glove and into right field. The winning run scored, and the Mets proceeded with the most joyous, improbable celebration ever seen. After this debacle, the outcome of Game 7 is predetermined: the Mets win 8-5. Buckner's wicket-splitting whiff is perhaps the most famous error in modern baseball history.

The drought continued. The Sox won the AL East Division in 1988 and 1990. And each time, were swept in the ALCS, 4-0. They won it again in 1995, after baseball had added a new round of playoffs, the Division Series. Again, they were swept, three games to none.

Or consider the Chicago Cubs. Founded in 1876, the Cubs won back-to-back World Series in 1907 and 1908. They then launched upon a century of such futility that their unofficial nickname was "the Lovable Losers."

The Cubs reached the World Series in 1918, but lost in four games, to the afore-mentioned Red Sox (who many assert only won the Series because the Cubs were slightly more bewitched than they.) The Cubs would make the Series again in '29, '32, '35, '38, and '45. And lose each time.

The Cubs would not return to the playoffs again for forty years. Until 1984, when a talented Cubs team won the NL East to face the San Diego Padres in a best-of-five series for the NL crown. They won Game 1 13-0, then Game 2, 4-2. They needed to win one of three games to go to the World Series. And they could not do it. The Padres swept the last three games.

The Cubbies would relive the frustration in 1989, losing the NLCS in five games. In 2003, they would again reach the league championship series and take a 3-1 lead in games, only to watch the Marlins win three in a row to take the pennant. These debacles would be interspersed with complete collapses in the Division Series in 1998, 2007, and 2008, failing to win a single game in any of them. In 2015, the Cubs would reach the NLCS once more. They would lose all four games.

The Cubs have their own Billy Buckner story: the legend of Steve Bartman. It was October 14, 2003, at Wrigley Field. The Cubs were playing the Marlins in the National League Championship Series – the winner would go on to the World Series. The Cubs had taken a three games to two lead and could clinch the series at home. In Game 6, Cubs ace Mark Prior baffled the Marlins batters, while Chicago had pushed across single runs in the first, sixth, and seventh. With a 3-0 lead, the Cubs were but six outs away from reaching the World Series for the first time in 58 years.

In the 8th, Prior got leadoff batter Mike Mordecai to fly out, but then Juan Pierre doubled. The next Marlins batter, Luis Castillo, on a 3-2 count, hit a lazy fly down the left field foul line near the stands. Left fielder Moises Alou camped out under it, timing his leap for what would have been the second out. And then a lifelong Cubs fan, Steve Bartman, reached out in an attempt to get the souvenir of his life. He didn't catch it. Instead, his bobble deflected the ball away from the waiting glove of Alou and onto the ground. The Cubs' vehement protests of interference fell on deaf ears. Instead of the second out, Castillo's pop fly was merely a foul ball, thanks to the overeager fingers of Steve Bartman.

The rest of the game is part of Cubs fans' collective history of agony. Rattled by the controversy and the long delay while the Cubs argued in vain for interference, Prior uncorked a wild pitch to the backstop. Not only did Pierre advance to third, but it was ball four to Castillo. First and third, one out. On a 0-2 pitch, the next batter, Ivan Rodriguez, singled, scoring Pierre. Next, Miguel Cabrera hit a high chopper to short, a sure out.

Except the ball bounced off the glove of Cubs shortstop Alex Gonzalez. Everyone was safe. Then the wheels fell completely off: a double, an intentional walk, a sacrifice fly, another intentional walk, a double, and a single. When Castillo finally and mercifully popped out to Mike Remlinger, the third pitcher for the Cubs that inning, the Marlins had scored eight runs. Just like the Red Sox after the Buckner incident in Game 6 in 1986, the shaken Cubs' fate in Game 7 was preordained. Kerry Wood, the Cubs' ace gave up seven runs. The Marlins won 9-6 and advanced to the World Series. Steve Bartman, faced with actual death threats, was forced into hiding.

Or let us pity the fans of the Cleveland Indians. Beginning life as the Cleveland Blues in 1901 (then, fleetingly, the Broncos, then the Naps), the Indians won a single World Series in 1920, and would never win another AL pennant again until 1948, when they went on to win the Series over the Boston Braves. The Indians would repeat as AL champs in '54, but then get swept in the Series by the New York Giants in four straight.

Then four decades would go by during which the Indians would not even get a whiff of the playoffs. Finally, in 1995, the Indians not only made the playoffs, but won the American League Championship to face the Atlanta Braves in the Series. They lost in six. Maddeningly, the

Braves won Game 1, Game 2, and Game 6, each by a single run. Since then, the Indians have lost the following playoffs:

- '96 Division Series
- '97 World Series (in Game 7)
- '98 ALCS
- '99 Division Series,
- 2001 Division Series
- '07 ALCS
- one-game wild card playoff in 2013
- World Series in 2016 (in Game 7, in extra innings)
- Division Series in 2017
- Division Series in 2018.

In the 1987 baseball preview issue of Sports Illustrated magazine, the cover featured the Indians and stated boldly: "Believe it! Cleveland is the best team in the American League!" Believe it or not – the Indians lost 101 games that year, the worst record in baseball.

Indians fans know well the myth of Tantalus: they have lived it. In '99, they won the first two games of the five-game ALDS. They lost the next three games. In 2001, they took a two game to one lead in the Division Series. They lost the next two games. In 2007, they took a three games to one lead in the ALCS. They lost the next three games. In 2013, they faced a one-game wild card game to advance to the ALDS. They lost. In 2017, they took a 2-1 lead in the five game ALDS. They lost the next two games. In other words, between 1999 and 2017, the Indians played three times in a Game 5 in a five game series, twice in a Game 7 in a seven game series, and once in a one-game playoff. And they lost them all.

Fans of the Red Sox, Cubs, and Indians, punished by decades-long absences from the World Series and debacles that were, statistically, almost impossible, spent year after year pondering how these endless fiascos could occur. Why were these teams so snake-bit? How could Billy

Buckner or Steve Bartman snatch victory away from franchises starved by half-centuries of disappointment after disappointment? How could the Indians lose every single elimination game they played, year after year after year?

These disasters seemed more appropriate to the Book of Job than the national pastime. The fans of these star-crossed teams examined the evidence, and reached the only possible conclusion that enlightened men of reason could: their teams were cursed.

For these teams, the diagnosis of a curse was easy. There simply could be no other explanation. The more pressing question – what was the source of the curse? And, perhaps more pragmatically, how could it be removed?

The source of the Red Sox curse was quite plain to all. There could only be one cause: Babe Ruth. After the 1919 season, the Red Sox's owner, Harry Frazee, had sold Ruth, the greatest player ever to play the game, to the New York Yankees for cash. According to the legend, the reason for the sale was that Frazee, who was not only a baseball owner but a theatrical producer, needed the money to launch a new musical, *No, No, Nanette*.[4]

The trade had radically opposite effects on the two teams. The Yankees, formerly a team of mediocrity, swiftly became perennial league champions and the most successful baseball franchise in history. They had never won a championship before Ruth. Since the trade with Boston, they have forty American League pennants, and have won the World Series 27 times. On the other hand, the Red Sox became, well, the Red Sox. Their 1918 World Series win, a mere year before the Ruth trade, would blink like a neon sign to remind the faithful of the source of the curse.

The Bambino theory is sound – virtually unchallengeable. There is only one Babe Ruth. Legend has it that, during World War II, American GIs would yell at opposing Japanese soldiers, "F--- Hirohito." The

---

4. For more on the Babe Ruth curse, see *The Curse of the Bambino* by Dan Shaughnessy.

Japanese loved their Emperor, and this outrage, against He who ruled the Empire by divine right, could not be allowed to go unanswered. But since the Americans had no beloved royal figure for them to curse in return, the Japanese soldiers were stumped. "F--- President Roosevelt" didn't exactly roll off with the tongue or provide the same weapons-grade insult to the Americans. Instead, they fixed upon an insult to the closest thing the GIs had to royalty: "F---- Babe Ruth." After all, the Babe was, in essence, America's version of royalty.

Trading the Babe – to pay for a musical! – was intolerable to the baseball gods, as it should be. No doubt, the Red Sox deserved the curse.

The curse of the Cubs, while no less real than the Red Sox's, is of less certain genesis. The Cubs could not point to the trade of an Olympian like Ruth (as noted, there was only one). After some study, Cubs fans opined that the curse must have occurred sometime around the last time the Cubs were successful – 1945. They fastened upon an incident in the 1945 World Series involving the Cubs' discrimination against a fan, on the basis of not race, or gender, or age, but species.

William Sianis owned a Chicago bar called the Billy Goat Tavern. Sianis also owned a pet goat named Murphy that served as the bar's mascot. For some reason, Sianis wished to bring Murphy to Game 4 of the 1945 World Series, and apparently bought him a ticket. But fans complained about Murphy's stench, and Sianis and Murphy were asked to leave. Sianis reportedly said: "You are going to lose this World Series and you are never going to win another World Series again." (Sianis was also Greek, and Greeks know curses. Just ask Sophocles.) And thus was born the Curse of the Billy Goat.[5]

Across town, the Chicago White Sox endured similar misfortune. In 1919, certain of the Chicago White Sox took bribes from gamblers, most notably Arnold Rothstein of New York, to throw the World Series. The exact scope of the conspiracy, and which of the White Sox were in on it, and which were mere dupes or innocent, has been hotly debated

---

5. For more on Murphy and Sianis, see *The Billy Goat Curse: Losing and Superstition in Cubs Baseball Since World War II* by Gil Bogen.

for decades. But the fact remains that some of the White Sox, or "Black Sox" as they have since been known, agreed to let their opponents, the Reds, win the World Series. Commissioner Kennesaw Mountain Landis banned eight of the White Sox players for life, including one of the greatest players of all time, "Shoeless Joe" Jackson. Jackson's lifetime batting average of .356 is third best in baseball history. He remains out of the Hall of Fame due to Landis's ban.

And thus was born the curse of the Black Sox. After that shameful World Series, the Pale Hose were, like the Israelites, forty years in the wilderness before returning to the World Series in 1959. They lost. They would not make the playoffs again for another 24 years. They lost in the ALCS. Another decade of failure, then they returned to the ALCS again in 1993. They lost. They would not win another World Series until 2005 – 83 years of woe.

Cleveland Indians fans have taken their cue from the Red Sox's Curse of the Bambino. The Indians' Bambino? Rocky Colavito.[6] Colavito, the Tribe's beloved slugger, was the AL home run king in 1959, with 42 home runs. The Indians, allegedly disgruntled by Colavito's rising salary demands, traded him in 1960 to Detroit for Harvey Kuenn, two days before opening day. Although Kuenn was the AL batting champ with a scalding .353 batting average, he lacked Colavito's power, as well as his fan appeal. Indians general manager Frank Lane claimed he had merely "traded hamburger for steak." But according to Indians lore, all the Indians' woes run from the dumping of Rocky Colavito. After that trade, they went 35 seasons without a World Series appearance. In 1995, they went to the Series, only to lose to the Atlanta Braves in six. Since 1995, they have returned to the World Series twice – in 1997 and 2016. Both times they lost, both times in Game 7.

The most entertaining curse does not even belong to an American baseball team, but to the Hanshin Tigers of the Japanese Central League.

---

6. For more on the bedeviled Indians, see *The Curse of Rocky Colavito: A Loving Look at a 33-Year Slump*, by Terry Pluto. The book was written in 1994; it's now a 57-year slump.

Powered by the slugging of American expat Randy Bass,[7] the Tigers won the Japan Championship Series in 1985 (Japan's World Series). It was the first and only Series win for the Tigers in their fifty-year history.

How would you celebrate such the end of a half-century drought? Well, exuberant Hanshin fans celebrated by having each Tiger player impersonated by a lookalike fan, dressing those fans in Tiger uniforms and having them, one by one, leap off the local Ebisu Bridge into the Dōtonbori canal.

Unfortunately, the celebrants ran into a quandary. No Hanshin fan was available who resembled the Caucasian Randy Bass. So they seized upon the best available simulacrum: a plastic statue of Colonel Harlan Sanders, the founder of Kentucky Fried Chicken. He was white, like Bass, and bearded, like Bass. It seemed like a logical replacement to the riotous fans.

Pried from his place of honor in front of a local KFC restaurant, the Colonel was dressed in a Bass jersey, and, with great ceremony, thrown off the bridge into the river. But he would get his revenge. After the Colonel's plunge into the waters of the Dōtonbori canal, the Hanshin Tigers then finished either last or next to last in the league for the next 18 years. They have returned only once to the Japan Series, in 2003. Local KFCs bolted their Colonel Sanders statues to the ground, but it was an unnecessary precaution, as the Tigers lost to the Fukuoka Daiei Hawks in seven games.

Dejected Tigers fans, desperate to assuage the Colonel's displeasure, have even sent divers down, repeatedly, to rescue him from his watery abode, without success. Then, on March 10, 2009, construction divers, working in the canal on the foundations for a new canal path, spotted

---

7. Bass had kicked around the American major leagues for six years, averaging around fifty at-bats a season, and compiling a paltry .212 batting average. But once in Japan, he became a fearsome slugger. In 1985, the year described above, Bass hit 54 homers. The Japanese league record was 55, held by Sadaharu Oh, Japan's version of Babe Ruth. On the last game of the regular season, with a chance to tie or break Oh's record, Bass never got a chance. He was intentionally walked each time by the opposing pitcher for the Yomiuri Giants. The manager for the Giants? Sadaharu Oh.

what they thought was a corpse. It was in fact the algae-covered torso of the Colonel, and they raised him, in chunks, from his three decades in Japan's version of Davy Jones's Locker. While most of the statue was recovered, his eye glasses and his left hand still dwell somewhere at the bottom of the canal. Until all of the Colonel is retrieved, the legend goes, there will be no joy in Kansai.

Baseball fans of course know that two of these curses have been broken in spectacular fashion. In 2004, the Boston Red Sox, down three games to none to the hated Yankees, won four straight to win the AL Championship. They were, and remain, the only team ever to come back from a 0-3 deficit to win a seven-game playoff series. They won Game 7 at Yankee Stadium to dance and pile on each other on the mound at the House that Ruth Built. If that's not the way to break the Curse of the Bambino, I don't know one. They've since won another three World Series titles. The specter of the Bambino has definitely been laid to rest.

Likewise, the hapless Cubs won the 2016 pennant, and then won the 2016 World Series in likely the most incredible Game 7 ever played. They won in extra innings, 8-7 against....the Cleveland Indians. Someone of course had to win and break their curse. But the fact that it required a seesaw, extra-inning Game 7, a four and a half hour marathon, with a rain delay thrown in just for giggles, proves the curses are real: the baseball gods didn't want either team to win. While the Curse of the Goat may have been lifted, Rocky Colavito still haunts the Indians.

The final exorcism of these curses doesn't dispel the reality of their existence. Eighty-six years passed between the Red Sox winning the World Series in 1918 (again, let us remember, against the equally cursed Cubs) and their 2004 World Series win, with dozens of exquisitely painful exits from contention during that span. The Curse of the Black Sox lasted eighty-seven years. One hundred and eight years passed between the Cubs winning the 1908 World Series and their 2016 World Series championship (against the equally bedeviled Indians), with scores of soul-crushing brushes with triumph in that interim. The Indians' skein still stands intact at seventy years of futility.

But, you say, how can the Nationals, who have only been in existence since 2005, be legitimately compared to these teams with such pedigrees of failure? Even given the unprecedented fiasco of Max's Scherzer's Inning from Hell on Black Thursday, how can that compare to the Red Sox's or White Sox's nearly nine decades of disaster, the Indians' seven decades, the Cubs' century? The Nats had one heartbreaking loss – how is that a "curse"?

Doubters of the Curse of the Nationals can scoff all they want. If they will follow me down the painful Memory Lane of the Nationals' seasons of despair, the scoffers will learn that the Nats can hold their own against any of the famous "cursed" teams.

So let us relive the misery and the woe that is the Nationals' wretched playoff history. It's not for the faint of heart.

CHAPTER 3

Are The Nationals Cursed? Oh, Brother.

WHEN THE NATIONALS MOVED TO Washington in 2005, the team was owned by Major League Baseball. In an unprecedented move, the failing Montreal franchise had been taken into trust by MLB in 2002. The Expos' entire payroll and management was sponsored and controlled by the rest of the two leagues. Each baseball team was effectively paying 1/29th of the Expos' operational costs, just to prevent the team from fading into oblivion. Rather than allowing the Expos to die, baseball had made them, in effect, wards of the state.

The situation was unsatisfactory to all. No team yearned to pay not only its own costs, but the costs of a competitor as well. The issue of Major League Baseball itself directing the player personnel decisions of the Expos, making trades, negotiating contracts, and drafting prospects, posed countless conflicts of interest.

So MLB decided that Washington would be the new home of the Expos. Astonishingly, the Nation's Capital had been without the National Pastime for 34 years. The original Washington Senators, founded in 1901, had decamped to Minnesota in 1961 to become the Twins. In a strange twist, without missing a beat, Washington had been immediately given a new expansion franchise, also called the Senators. The new Senators had lasted a mere ten years in Washington before also absconding in 1971, this time to become the Texas Rangers. After those failures, Major League Baseball had passed over the District repeatedly when awarding expansion franchises to Seattle and Toronto in 1977, to Denver and Miami in 1993, and to Phoenix and Tampa Bay in 1998.

The original Washington Senators were bad. In 1909, they lost 110 games and finished an astonishing 56 games out of first place. Ten times in their history, they finished 40 games or more out of first place (in a 154 game season, mind you). While they had been to the World Series twice in the early 1920s, winning in 1925, they had done so on the broad back of Walter Johnson, probably the greatest starting pitcher in baseball history. Despite that, and another AL pennant in 1933, the Senators were for the most part a national laughingstock.

They were bad. So bad that San Francisco Chronicle columnist Charley Dryden famously converted President George Washington's eulogy – "Washington: First in war, first in peace, and first in the hearts of his countrymen"—to accommodate the Senators: "Washington: First in war, first in peace, and last in the American League." So bad that another Broadway musical was spawned, *Damn Yankees*, whose plot was that the only thing which could turn the Senators into winners was Satan himself.

But the Senators didn't tease their fans with hopes of pennants or World Series, which the baseball gods would then dash in some theretofore never-before-seen way. They were merely continually putrid – deservedly putrid – and Senators fans knew their team was putrid.

More important, the Senators, abysmal, as they were, were not the team that became the Nationals. We cannot tack the failures of the Senators onto the Nats just because they shared the same city. The established rules of sport curses don't permit it. If a hex haunted the Senators, it traveled to Minnesota.

But don't worry: the Nationals can take care of the curse all by themselves.

When the Expo-Nationals arrived in Washington in 2005, they would continue to be owned by the MLB trusteeship for another eighteen months. MLB provided the Nats with a veteran GM, Jim Bowden, a veteran skipper in Frank Robinson, and a moderate payroll. And lo and behold, the Nats finished 81-81, a respectable record for an orphaned franchise.

In bringing the Expos to Washington, baseball intended to quickly solicit bids for local ownership of the team and end the MLB financial trusteeship as soon as possible. But the bidding was not held as a true auction; rather, the purchase price was fixed by MLB at a discounted $400 million. With several consortiums bidding, MLB selected the Lerner family, native real estate magnates, as the next owners of the Washington Nationals.

Taking possession of their purchase mid-season in 2006, the Lerners immediately slashed the team's payroll from $63 million to $37 million. The Nats' new management clearly had no interest in fielding a competitive team in the early years of ownership. As one would expect, the Nationals plummeted in the standings, finishing dead last in the NL East in 2006. And in 2008. And 2009. And 2010.

But slowly, the Lerners starting spending money. In 2009, entranced by agent Scott Boras's silver tongue, they gave No. 1 draft pick Stephen Strasburg a $7.5 million signing bonus – the largest ever up until that time. When they acquired the 2010 No. 1 pick, they selected Bryce Harper, also a Boras client, and conferred a $6.2 million signing bonus, also a new record for a position player. Before the 2011 season, the Nats signed free agent outfielder Jayson Werth to a seven-year, $125 million contract, the largest the Lerners had ever approved. They clearly meant business. By 2012, the Nationals' payroll was a quite respectable $92 million.

And what did it get them?

2012

The newly free-spending Nationals got off to a hot start, winning 14 of their first 20 games. But three weeks into the season, manager Davey Johnson got his wish. The Nats' heralded phenom, Bryce Harper, was brought up to the majors and made his major league debut on April 28.

This was the moment Nats fans had dreamed of: the Big Kid in the bigs. Since he had appeared on the cover of Sports Illustrated as "The Chosen One" as a high school sophomore, one of the hottest topics in baseball was which team would be lucky enough to land Harper. Even before Harper had inked his first major league contract, comparisons were being made to Hall of Fame players. And when the Nationals took him in the 2010 draft at number one overall, Nats fans lost their collective minds.

He was joining Stephen Strasburg, the previous year's No. 1 overall, and veterans Ryan Zimmerman and Ian Desmond, who provided both offense and defense on the left side of the diamond. Furthermore, the Nats had picked up All-Star Gio Gonzalez in the offseason. The years of accepting a last place finish were clearly over.

Despite losing Werth to a broken arm in early May, the Nationals took the division lead for good on May 22 and never looked back. Gonzalez was dominating, finishing with a 2.89 ERA and a league-leading 21 wins, and the Nats led all major league teams with 98 wins. That meant they would host the National League Division Series against the wild card St. Louis Cardinals. Strasburg was unavailable for the playoffs; he had undergone Tommy John surgery in 2011, and due to fears of re-injury, had been shut down in early September after reaching an innings limit. But Werth was back and healthy, and first baseman Adam LaRoche was having a career year at the plate.

In Game 1 in St. Louis, the Nationals would score two runs in the 8th against the Cardinals' bullpen to pull out a 3-2 win. But game 2 starter Jordan Zimmermann, despite a sparkling 2.94 ERA in the regular season, was lit up like a Christmas tree by the Cardinals in a 12-4 bloodbath.

On to game 3, tied at one apiece. Nats' starter Edwin Jackson gave up four quick runs, and the Washington bullpen was no help either. A Cardinals win, 8-0. Now facing elimination, the Nationals got a six-inning gem from Ross Detwiler, who gave up a single unearned run. The all-hands-on-deck bullpen put up zeroes in the 7th, 8th and 9th. With the game tied 1-1 in the ninth inning, Jayson Werth provided perhaps the most memorable moment in Nationals playoff history. On a 3-2 count, Werth hit a leadoff home run to win the game. Werth was mobbed at the plate in a celebration that Nats fans still remember. Now, with momentum clearly on their side, the Nats would be playing at home the very next day for the deciding Game 5. With their 21-game winner Gonzalez on full rest, Washington fans liked their chances – a lot.

Magically, Game 5 unfolded like a dream for the Nats. In the first inning, the Nats hitters knocked around Cards ace Adam Wainwright like the proverbial rented mule: a Werth double, then a Harper triple, followed by a Zimmerman homer. In the bottom of the third, the same: a leadoff homer by Harper, followed by Zimmerman doubling. After Adam LaRoche struck out, Michael Morse hit a blast into the outfield seats: 6-0 Nats! With Gio on the mound, the game was in the bag. The Nats were going to win and advance to the Championship Series.

Only it wasn't in the bag. Gio immediately spit the bit. He gave up a single run in the 4th, and then the wheels fell completely off in the fifth. The Cardinals led off with a double, then a single. Gonzalez then walked the next batter to load the bases. Next, Gonzalez threw a wild pitch to allow another run to score, and reloaded the bases with a walk. After a groundout, Gonzalez recorded another walk, pushing another runner across. A flyout by Molina ended the inning with the bases loaded. One inning, two hits, three walks, and a wild pitch. The Cardinals still trailed 6-3, but, at 99 pitches, Gonzalez was done.

The Nats held them scoreless in the sixth, but Edwin Jackson, pitching in relief, gave up a run on an RBI groundout by Matt Holiday in the seventh, cutting the Nats' lead to 6-4. Washington went to their stellar setup man, Tyler Clippard in the 8th. In 2011, Clippard had made the All-Star team as a setup man, which is hard to do. Clippard threw gas – he had recorded 32 of 37 save opportunities in this season, only to yield the role to Drew Storen later in the year. In 72-plus innings, he had given up only seven home runs all year.

The first batter he faced was Daniel Descalso. Descalso was what is known as a banjo hitter: the ball comes off his bat as if he were swinging a banjo rather than a club of Northern white ash. That year, in 426 plate appearances, he had hit a grand total of four home runs. His slugging percentage in 2012 was .324, the lowest of any Cardinal position player on the playoff roster. Other than pitchers, there was no less dangerous hitter that the Cardinals had on their team.

Guess what. Descalso hit a home run. Clippard got out of the inning with no more damage, but the lead was down to a single run. In the bottom of the eighth, the Nationals' bats, silent for several innings, awakened, and they strung together three singles to score an insurance run.

Now, with a two run lead, closer Drew Storen entered the game. He needed only to retire three Cardinals to win the game and the series. After a brilliant 2011, recording 43 saves as the Nats' closer, he had spent the first half of the season on the disabled list. But after his return in mid-July, Storen had gradually regained the closer's role from Clippard. He was good – in 37 appearances, he had recorded a 2.37 ERA with four saves and a single blown save.

The first batter was the dangerous Carlos Beltran, and Storen gave up a double. Storen then got the next two batters on a groundout and a punchout swinging. The Nats needed one out. A single, lone, solitary out.

Statistically, the sabermetricians tell us that at this point in the game the Nationals have a 96% chance of winning the game. But, as it turns out, they don't in fact. Storen walked Yadier Molina. Then he walked David Freese. Bases loaded. Up to bat: the mighty Daniel Descalso. The banjo hitter. He singled, scoring Beltran and Molina. The game is tied.

Still, in search of that single out, Storen faced Pete Kozma, the Cardinals No. 8 hitter. Kozma was a September callup for the Cardinals. He had at this point 89 major league at bats in his entire life, so few that he would still be a rookie the following year. He had two hits in eleven at-bats in this NLDS. He could not be a threat to Storen.

Storen stared in at Kozma, and dealt. Called first strike. He fired a second pitch. Called strike two. On the third pitch, Descalso took off for second. If he were to be caught, the inning would be over. But the throw was late, and Descalso stood at second. Two pitches later, Kozma unleashed a drive to right field. It fell in for a single, and both Freese and Descalso scored to take a 9-7 lead. Storen struck out Jason Motte, the pitcher, but it's over. The stunned Nats went down meekly, 1-2-3, in the bottom of the ninth, and headed home for the winter.

These are the things that had to happen to lose this game:

- The Nats squander a six-run lead.
- Gonzalez, the winningest pitcher in the league, comes unglued in the fifth.
- In the 8th, with two strikes, Daniel Descalso, a .227 hitter with no power, hits a home run off Tyler Clippard, one of the best relievers in baseball.
- In the 9th, with two outs, Storen walks not one, but two batters.
- Still with two outs, Descalso, the aforementioned .227 hitter, singles off Storen.
- Still with two outs, *with two strikes*, Pete Kozma, a last minute afterthought to the Card's playoff roster, who has been in the majors for a month, hits a two-run single off Drew Storen to win the game.

2013

The Nationals fans and local sports writers spent the winter agonizing over Storen's ability to finish that two-out, two-strike situation. Stunned as the Nats were, they went out to make themselves better in the offseason. They picked up the solid and reasonably priced Denard Span from the Twins to patrol center field. They re-signed LaRoche, and signed Dan Haren, a durable back-end starter.

Most important, they had learned their lesson. They needed a capital-C Closer. So they signed Rafael Soriano, fresh off a 42-save season for the Yankees, so that the Storen disaster would never happen again.

After their phenomenal 98-win season in 2012, the collective wisdom of the sports world said that the Nationals would go to the World Series. Vegas made them the odds favorite to win it all, at 6-1. Sports Illustrated's baseball preview issue picked the Nats to win the Series:

the cover featured Stephen Strasburg as "Mr. October." Expectations were sky-high – manager Davey Johnson said it was "the World Series or bust."

And the baseball gods heard, and granted Davey's wish: bust it was. The Nationals were in first place for the first five games of the season. They lost the lead on April 7, and never saw first place again. The arch-rival Atlanta Braves would beat them all year, taking 13 out of 19 head-to-head games. Before the end of July, the Nationals were an unthinkable 10 games behind the division leading Braves, and never threatened again. Soriano would close 43 games, but none in the playoffs.

2014

Despite the shocking results of 2013, the Nationals front office hadn't lost faith. It had to be a fluke. To bolster their disappointing rotation, they traded for the soft-tossing but effective Doug Fister, but in general, the Nats were content to stand pat with their 2013 roster. They also added Matt Williams, the former Giants third baseman, as their new skipper to replace Davey Johnson.

The baseball pundits generally agreed. To them, 2013 was an inexplicable and unrepeatable outlier. For the second consecutive year, Sports Illustrated picked the Nationals to not only win the pennant, but to win the World Series.

But as the season started, the Nats struggled to find their footing. On Memorial Day, they were in third place, and at 25-26 a game below .500. But in June they went 17-11. Then 14-10 in July, and a sizzling 19-10 in August. They capped off September with a gobsmacking 19-8 run, leaving the second place Braves seventeen games back.

The Nats finished with 96 wins and were red-hot going into the playoffs. On the last game of the season, as a cherry on top, Jordan Zimmermann pitched his first career no-hitter, which reserve outfielder Stephen Souza had saved on a spectacular diving catch in the left-center gap.

Yes. It was their year. Their pitching was phenomenal – a league-leading 3.03 ERA – and, this year, Strasburg was available for the play-offs. They were not going to be denied this time.

As the team with the best record, they would host a five-game series against the winner of the wildcard game. San Francisco smoked the Pirates, 8-0, to win the honor of facing Washington at Nationals Park.

In Game 1, the Giants sent their ace Jake Peavy to the mound to face Strasburg. Peavy baffled the Nats' bats for five and two-thirds, giving up only two hits and no runs. Strasburg was not as dominating, giving up eight hits in five, but able to wriggle out of major damage. When Strasburg left the game after five, he had given up only two runs, one unearned on a passed ball by Wilson Ramos. The Giants then tacked on another in the seventh: 3-0. The Nationals would score only two runs, both on solo home runs in the seventh. In the eighth, when the Nats got the tying run to second, the Giants' bullpen held on. First game to the Giants.

Game 2: the Giants' Tim Hudson versus the Nats' Jordan Zimmerman. The game quickly settled into a classic pitcher's duel. The Nats tallied a single run in the third, while Zimmermann continued to pitch brilliantly. As he took the mound for the ninth inning, up 1-0, he had given up only three hits, and none since the third inning. He had struck out six and walked one.

Zimmermann struck out Matt Duffy, the leadoff batter, and induced an easy flyout to center from Gregor Blanco. He needed one out to close out a complete game shutout.

And he walked the next batter, Joe Panik. Zimmermann had thrown only 100 pitches. But rather than let him face the next batter, Buster Posey, manager Matt Williams came out and signaled to the bullpen for... Drew Storen.

The idea wasn't all that crazy. Storen had worked his way back from the 2012 disaster to earn the Nats' closing role once again. He had been perhaps the best reliever in the league that season, recording a minuscule ERA of 1.12 in 65 appearances. Meanwhile, Soriano had not performed like the reliable closer the Nats had expected. Once elevated into the closer role, Storen had tallied 10 consecutive saves in 10 consecutive appearances in September – all without allowing a single run.

But the crowd was clearly uneasy with the decision. Zimmermann, his no-hitter of last week fresh in everyone's mind, had been cruising all game. Nor, despite Storen's dominance all year, had they forgotten his 2012 playoff collapse. There was a smattering of boos as Williams took the ball from Zimmermann. Still, there was only one out to get.

The booers were immediately vindicated. Posey drove Storen's first pitch into center field. Now with runners on first and second, Storen faced the Giants third baseman, Pablo Sandoval. On the second pitch, Sandoval laced a double to left – Panik scored to tie the game, and Posey was gunned down at home trying to add on. Tie game. It had happened again.

What followed that second Storen failure was the longest playoff game in the history of baseball, an 18-inning slog in the bone-chilling October night. The Nationals' and Giants' respective bullpens would match inning for inning, zero for zero.

From the 9th inning to the 17th – the length of an entire second game – the home team Nats needed to score but a single run to win the game. And for those nine innings, the Nats batters failed to do it. Finally, in the top of the 18th, the Nats' Tanner Roark gave up a first-pitch home run to Brandon Belt.[8] The Nats went down meekly in the bottom half of the frame, and in a game lasting six hours and twenty-three minutes, disaster had struck again. The Giants had swept the first two games at Washington.

Now each game was an elimination game for the Nats. They refused to quit. In Game 3, behind Fister's seven shutout innings, the Nats won, 4-1. In Game 4, Gio Gonzalez again took the ball, ready to slay the ghosts of 2012's Game 5. But Gio's nerves were raw. In the first, he gave up consecutive singles, but retired Sandoval on a flyout to end the inning. In

---

8. The author left in the 17th. He pleads extenuating circumstances: he was in joint custody of two fourth graders who were wearing shorts, with temperatures in the forties, a stiff breeze, and it was midnight on a school night.

the second, after Brandon Crawford singled, the Giants' Juan Perez hit a tapper back to the mound, a tailor-made double play ball. But the ball clanked off the overeager Gonzalez and trickled into the infield grass. Everybody safe.

Next up, the pitcher, Ryan Vogelsong, who squared around to bunt. He dropped it to the third base side of the infield. Both Gonzalez and third baseman Rendon started for it, looked at each other, paused, and started for it again. The ball rolled to a stop on the ground. Everybody safe again.

The rattled Gonzalez continued to misfire. Now, with the bases loaded, he walked in a run on four consecutive balls. An RBI groundout led to another Giant run, and the Nats trailed 2-0.

The Nats would get one back in the top of the fifth. Then, in the top of the 7th, Bryce Harper, quiet all series, launched a massive solo shot off Hunter Strickland into McCovey Cove. The Nats dugout went nuts – tie game.[9]

Hardly had the exuberance faded when the Nats coughed it up again. In the bottom, the Nats brought out Matt Thornton to pitch. After recording an out, he gave up back-to-back singles to Panik and Posey. The Nats went to Aaron Barrett. Barrett then walked the next batter to load the bases. Then facing Sandoval, Barrett threw one to the backstop to allow Panik to score, and the Giants led, 3-2.

It was almost worse. With first base now open, Barrett, while attempting to intentionally walk the next batter, threw another wild pitch to the screen. Posey raced home, only to be tagged out on an incredibly lucky, no-look throw to the plate by Ramos to Barrett covering home.

And that was the final score. The Nats went quietly in the 8th and 9th, and the Giants won the series, 3-1.

---

9. So nuts in fact that Hunter Strickland would nurse a grudge for over 2 ½ years. When he faced Harper in a regular season game in May 2017, Strickland, in revenge for what he thought was Harper's over-effusive celebration, drilled Harper with his first pitch. That ignited a bench-clearing donnybrook, which culminated in three Giants teammates physically carrying the berserking Strickland from the field.

2015

The Nationals had had it. Stung by tantalizing loss after tantalizing loss, year after year, they went out and got the free agent prize of the winter, Max Scherzer. The Nats lineup looked simply ridiculous. Some baseball writers opined that the starting rotation of Scherzer, Strasburg, Zimmerman, Gonzalez, and Fister might be the greatest starting rotation in the entire history of baseball. There's simply no way the Nats can fail to win the World Series now.

Yet not only do the Nationals not win the World Series, *they don't even make the playoffs*. While Bryce Harper has a simply monster season, winning the NL MVP, regulars Werth, Desmond, and Ryan Zimmerman experience season-long slumps. Of the Nationals' best position players, six of the eight spend significant time on the disabled list. Both rookie center fielder Michael Taylor and starting catcher Wilson Ramos play their positions all year and post identical batting averages: an anemic .229. There are many games where the Nationals seem to be playing with three to four automatic outs in their lineups.

The Nats took first place in the division in late June, but couldn't seem to shake the pesky Mets, always two or three games behind. Smelling some weakness in the Nats, the Mets traded away several prospects at the deadline to pick up a couple of solid bench players and Tyler Clippard, now an Oakland Athletic.

Shortly after these trades, the Mets suffered a mindboggling loss to the Padres, having led 7-1 after six innings and still losing, 8-7. Washington Post baseball writer Tom Boswell taunted the Mets on Twitter after this game.

> *RIP Mets..... -3 games. Fun team. Ain't gonna happen. Don't trade away good future. There is no "present."*

The baseball gods, who love to punish hubris, heard. The Nationals then came to New York for a three game series. New York swept, and just like that, the teams were tied for first place. The next day the Mets took the lead in the division; they wouldn't trail the rest of the year. The Mets would come to Washington again in early September, leading by four games. A Nats sweep would put them only one game out of first with three weeks to play. There was a sweep, but by the Mets. They left DC up seven games, the same lead they would finish the season with.

Unfortunately, the "fun team – ain't gonna happen" Mets... happened. And once again the Nats found themselves packing up their lockers in October, staring into the mirror, wondering what could possibly explain this unending string of catastrophes.

2016

The embarrassed Nationals front office held a housecleaning. Gone were Denard Span, Ian Desmond, Doug Fister, and Jordan Zimmermann. Gone too was the scapegoat Storen. Then the Nats went out and signed, from their nemeses the Mets, second baseman Daniel Murphy. Murphy's batting stance adjustment late in the 2015 season had turned him from a productive hitter into a hitting beast. Slaphitting Ben Revere, a career .295 hitter, was added to solve the leadoff spot, a perennial weakness.

Also, Tanner Roark was recalled from his exile to the bullpen. Roark had been arguably the Nationals' second most reliable starter in 2014, when he went 15-10 with an impressive ERA of 2.85. But despite these numbers, with the acquisition of Scherzer, Roark had been kicked to the bullpen, where he did not thrive. Now, Roark would start again.

They also fired Matt Williams as manager, and replaced him with Dusty Baker. Baker was not the Lerners' first choice. They wanted Bud Black, who was available and viewed as the pitching-savvy manager the Nats need. But when the Lerners offered Black a one-year contract, for less than half the going rate for experienced managers, the insulted Black cut off all further negotiations with the Lerners. He quickly signed a three-year deal to manage the Rockies. The Nats hurriedly signed Baker to cover up the embarrassment.

For a team trying to end years of failing to meet expectations, Baker is an odd choice. While he brings a respectable win-loss record as a manager, he's managed 20 seasons and has never won a World Series, and only one pennant. Worse, his resume is riddled with the sort of epic swoons that the Nats have experienced and want to end. In 1993, his Giants were leading the NL West by nine games in mid-August, only to choke in September and lose the division to the Braves by a single game. In 2002, the Baker-led Giants won the pennant, and were leading the Angels 3 games to 2 in the Series, with a 5-0 lead in Game Six. They lost Game Six, and then Game Seven. In 2003, Baker managed the Cubs and got them to the NLCS. Up three games to one, they lost three in a row to watch the Marlins go to the Series. In 2012, he was in charge of the Reds, who won 97 games and the NL Central. Facing the Giants in the NLCS, they won the first two games, then lost the next three to lose the series. In 2013, in contention for the NL Central crown, the same Reds lost the last five games of the regular season, and then the wild card game to the Pirates. Baker has been unemployed since.

Nonetheless, the 2016 Nats came out of the gate smoking, racking up a 16-7 record in April. The Murphy acquisition paid off, as he led the entire NL with a .985 OPS.[10] Wilson Ramos emerged as an offensive force, batting .307 with 22 homers. Scherzer was simply brilliant, going 20-7 with a 2.96 ERA, and Tanner Roark nearly as good, a mere 16-10 with a slightly better ERA of 2.83. Washington destroyed the NL East, maintaining the division lead for all but three days of the season.

They would finish eight games up, with a 95-67 record, second best in the league to the Cubs. This meant they would again host the NLDS, this time against the NL West winners, the LA Dodgers.

Game 1 was to be the Clash of the Titans: Scherzer versus Kershaw. Kershaw had put up an infinitesimal 1.69 ERA, only pitching half the season due to injury. Scherzer led the league in wins, innings pitched, and strikeouts.

Both pitchers were clearly tight to start the game. Kershaw gave up an uncharacteristic eight hits in five innings, while Scherzer was hittable

---

10. OPS is on-base percentage (known by its acronym of OBP) plus slugging percentage. On-base percentage reflects ability to get on base by any means, and slugging percentage reflects total bases averaged per at-bat. OPS is a commonly-used shorthand statistic to assess a player's complete offensive production.

too, giving up four runs in six innings. Only the starters gave up runs in this game: Scherzer four, and Kershaw three. First game to the Dodgers.

In Game 2, both starters, LA's Rich Hill and DC's Roark, suffered early exits, but the Nats' bats finally came alive. The result was a 5-2 Washington win. The series was tied at one apiece.

The Nats' bats stayed hot in Game 3. While Gio Gonzalez again pitched ineffectively, so did the Dodgers' Kenta Maeda. With the Nats nursing a 4-3 lead after eight, the Dodgers brought in their lights-out closer, Kenley Jansen. Leading off, Jayson Werth greeted him with a home run to left. Now it was Jansen's turn to implode. A walk, a hit batter, and a Ryan Zimmerman double made it 7-3, and it would end 8-3.

Up two games to one, the Nats need only win one of the two remaining games. One of those games, Game 5, will be pitched by Max Scherzer. The Dodgers, facing elimination in Game 4, have little choice by to turn to Kershaw.

Game 4 was a seesaw. Nats up, 1-0. Dodgers up, 2-1. Tied, 2-2. Dodgers up, 4-2. Dodgers up, 5-2. Then, in the seventh, Kershaw ran out of gas, and was pulled with the bases loaded, two outs. The Dodgers bullpen wasn't up to the task. A hit batter drove in another Washington run before Daniel Murphy hit a two-run single to tie the game at 5 apiece.

The Nats' bullpen, forced into early action when starter Joe Ross lost the strike zone in the third, pitched magnificently. For five innings, they had yielded but one run. Now, in the bottom of the eighth, Blake Treinen retired the first two batters, but he hit Andrew Toles. Andre Ethier and Chase Utley followed with two singles to give Los Angeles a 6-5 lead. Kenley Jansen, a man reborn, made no mistake this time: three Nationals came to the plate and three Nationals sat down in the ninth.

That loss brought the series to an even 2-2 split, but the Nats were the clear favorites in Game 5. First, they would be playing at home. Second, they'd be sending their ace, Scherzer, to the mound, while the Dodgers shot their bolt in Game 4 with Kershaw. LA had to turn to Rich Hill, who was ineffective in Game 2.

But Hill pitched well, giving up only a single run. Nonetheless, at the first sign of trouble, the Dodger manager, a nervous Dave Roberts, pulled him in the third with two outs.

Scherzer pitched a gem for six innings. Up 1-0, Scherzer grooved his first pitch of the seventh inning to Joc Pederson. Joc deposited it over the left field fence to tie the game. Dusty Baker came to the mound and lifted Scherzer for Marc "Scrabble" Rzepczynski. He walked the next batter. Baker went to the bullpen again, tapping Blake Treinen. Trienen promptly gave up a single to the next Dodger before retiring Charlie Culberson on a foul bunt attempt. Sammy Solis replaced Treinen and allowed a single from the Dodgers catcher, Carlos Ruiz, to score Howie Kendrick from second. Now down 2-1, Baker walked from the dugout a third time to summon Shawn Kelley. Justin Turner greeted Kelley with a triple to center, scoring both runners. 4-1, Dodgers.

The agony was not over. Chris Heisey, pinch-hitting for the Nats in the seventh, hit a two-run homer to close the gap to 4-3. It's an elimination game – win or go home. The Dodgers decided to pull out all the stops. They called in Jansen in the seventh inning, rather than holding him back for the ninth, his usual task. Jansen walked the first batter, but then retired the next three in order. He again shut down the Nats in the eighth. In the ninth, staring down the top of the Nationals order, he struck out Trea Turner before walking Harper and Werth. The tying run was in scoring position, and the Nats' stadium, already to a fan on their feet, erupted in a deafening roar.

It had not gone unnoticed that the Dodgers ace of aces, Kershaw, had pulled off his warmup jacket and was getting loose in the bullpen. Now the Dodgers played their last card, and Kershaw strolled to the mound to try to record the last two outs.

But the Nats were not dead yet. Kershaw has earned a reputation for failing to perform in big games. On top of that, he had not pitched well in the series; he was pulled in Game 1 after five mediocre innings and got tagged for an unthinkable five runs in Game 4. The Nationals had the tying run on second with only one out, and their best hitter, Daniel

Murphy at the plate. Murphy was destroying pitchers in this series; he had already recorded seven hits and six RBI. The Nats were not dead.

But Kershaw got Murphy to pop weakly to second base, and then it was down to utilityman Wilmer Difo. Kershaw blew a third strike fastball by the overmatched Difo, and the Nats had again failed to win a playoff series – in another Game 5 loss.

2017

Well, we've seen it, in the first chapter of this book – the incredible, unprecedented, inconceivably preposterous Scherzer debacle in game 5. The Nationals, with the entire series in play, put in their best pitcher in relief, handing the ball to Scherzer to finish off the game. It's the exclamation point on the Curse of the Nationals.

But we skipped to the cataclysm. We omitted the rest.

For example, Game 3. Scherzer takes the mound in Game 3 with the series tied at 1 apiece. He turns in a masterpiece, as usual. But the Cubs' Jose Quintana proves equally tough for the National hitters, surrendering only one run.

Max is cruising: through six innings, he has a no-hitter. In the seventh, he retires the leadoff batter, and then Ben Zobrist breaks up the no-hitter with a double. Dusty Baker comes to the mound and takes the ball from Scherzer. In comes Sammy Solis. His first batter flares a single to the gap in left. Zobrist scores, and the game is 1-1.

In the 8th, the Cubs got a second run on a walk, a sacrifice, and a single. 2-1, Cubs. Wade Davis closes out the heart of the order, 1-2-3. Max pitches a one-hitter, which ends in a 2-1 loss.

Now, the Nats need to win both remaining games. Tanner Roark is scheduled to pitch Game 4 for the Nats, leaving the only-if-necessary Game 5 for Stephen Strasburg. Despite Roark's solid 13-11 season, the Nats don't trust him with the entire season on the line.

But suddenly, the eternally snake-bit Nationals catch a huge, huge break. The baseball gods send a massive thunderstorm to Chicago, and Game 4 is postponed a day.

The Nationals' brain trust is ecstatic. Now Roark can be skipped. Strasburg, the Nats' No. 2 and in the midst of a Cy Young worthy season himself, can pitch Game 4. Gio Gonzalez will pitch Game 5. More important, lurking in the bullpen in Game 5 will be the nuclear weapon: Max Scherzer. He'll be on two days' rest, but the Nationals have the games lined up just like they want. Once they win Game 4, sometime in Game 5 in the fifth, sixth, or seventh inning, they're going to hand the ball to the best pitcher in the game, the man who just hurled six no-hit innings against this same Cubs team. It's a dream come true.

And suddenly, Tantalus awakens. Suddenly, just like that, Stephen Strasburg isn't feeling well.

Strasburg, a National since 2010, is one of the most enigmatic players in today's game. He is also one of the most injured. And for a panoply of ailments. In his first season, he blew out his elbow after only twelve starts, requiring Tommy John surgery. He missed virtually all of 2011. In 2012, as we have seen, the team shut him down in September, despite the Nationals advancing to the playoffs, when he hit a preset innings limit. He struggled in 2013, going 8-9. In the 2015 season alone, he went on the DL for problems with his 1) ankle, 2) shoulder, 3) neck, and 4) oblique muscles; he made only 23 starts. In 2016, more of the same, missing a dozen starts and the playoffs to boot. There is not-so-muted grumbling among the Washington faithful that most of Strasburg's maladies are between his ears.

Now, about to pitch in his most important game for the Nats ever, he is complaining he can't go. The alleged culprit? He claims to have an allergic reaction to "mold." And the Nationals' fans go from ecstasy back to agony.

The quiet grousing about Strasburg's hypochondria now reached a roar. Fans are apoplectic: how can our stud pitcher, he of the $175 million contract, refuse to take the ball in this elimination game? Baseball writers and ex-players agreed. Short of having his pitching arm amputated, there was no illness that could excuse this no-show. Strasburg's illness and intestinal fortitude were openly questioned on every TV and radio sports talk show in America.

But wait: on the day of the game, Strasburg says that his symptoms have improved, and he wants the ball. Roark is scratched again, and Strasburg starts Game 4 as planned. Washington fans aren't having it – they're hanging crepe all over town. Either Strasburg's actually sick, in which case we lose, or he's a wimp, in which case we lose. Either way, the Nats are doomed to failure, says the current wisdom.

Strasburg pitches the game of his life, a 5-0 win that puts his critics to rest for good, a seven inning, three-hit, twelve-strikeout masterpiece. From the ashes, Nationals fans collectively rise. We cannot lose – we got Max in the bullpen.

And out of the ashes, back into the ashes, as the Inning from Hell alights to torture the Nats faithful yet again, this time in exquisitely unprecedented fashion.

For the unconvinced, to sum up the most salient evidence for the Curse of the Nationals:

- They have played four playoff series in the last six years. They've lost each one.
- Of the four playoff series lost, they've lost three of them in Game 5, and one in Game 4.
- Of those four final game losses, three were by a single run.
- They've lost twelve playoff games in all. Of those twelve, they've lost nine by a single run.
- They've lost four of the playoff games in the other team's last at-bat.
- In three of those last at-bat losses, the winning run was scored with two outs; twice, with two outs and two strikes.
- In their last appearance, the best pitcher in baseball became the answer to an absurd trivia question demonstrating the four ways to get on base without putting the ball into play: walk, dropped third strike, catcher's interference, and hit by pitch.

Skeptics may insist that, regardless of the undebatable awfulness of the Nationals' playoff woes, that they simply do not possess the pedigree for a Curse. They're too young. Long-suffering fans of the Red Sox, the Cubs, or the Indians may say, "Our agony lasted *decades*. You Nats fans are complaining about *five years of disasters*. Heck, you've only existed since 2005. You don't have the resume for a Curse, you poseurs."

Except it's not five years of disasters. It's much, much more. It turns out that the Curse of the Nationals predates the Nationals – by a lot. In fact, even the Scherzer debacle wasn't a first for the Nationals. Eerily, virtually the exact same thing had happened to the Nationals exactly thirty-six years before – when they were the Montreal Expos.

CHAPTER 4

BLUE MONDAY

IN 1961, MAJOR LEAGUE BASEBALL did something it had not done since the turn of the century. It added new teams. While for six decades baseball had consisted of an eight-team American League and an eight-team National League, no more. 1961 saw the addition of the Los Angeles Angels and a new Washington Senators team to the American League. In 1962, the Mets and the Houston Astros (who would wear the "Colt .45s" nickname for their first three years) joined the National League.

Then, in 1969, major league baseball added four more expansion teams, which included for the first time a team that was not based in the United States. Montreal would be the first international franchise in major league history. [11]

An odd choice? At first blush, perhaps, but Montreal had some baseball history. In fact, Canadians claim that the first ever documented baseball game was played, not in America, but in Canada, on June 4, 1838, at Beachville, Ontario, years before the New York Knickerbockers debuted the American version in 1845. Montreal proudly sported a professional minor league club dating back to 1897, known as the Royals. While that club folded, a new minor league team with the same name was founded in the late 1920s. In 1939, the Brooklyn Dodgers sought out

---

11. The other additions were the Kansas City Royals (AL), the San Diego Padres (NL), and the Seattle Pilots (AL) – not to be confused with the Mariners. The Pilots, after one bad season, fled to Milwaukee, where they became the Brewers.

the Royals, an established International League franchise, and turned it into their top minor league level.

As a result, almost every great homegrown Dodger for the next twenty years would come through Montreal as a Royal: Duke Snider, Don Drysdale, Don Newcombe, Roy Campanella. Sparky Anderson and Tommy Lasorda were Royals; so was Roberto Clemente. After leaving the Negro leagues, Jackie Robinson played his first professional game as a Royal in 1946; he would leap to the Dodgers the next year and break the color barrier in baseball.

But when the Royals died in 1960, Montreal was suddenly *sans* baseball. They needed a team, and a few years later, Major League Baseball, to the surprise of many, was willing to give them one.

It wasn't a crazy idea. In 1969, Montreal had some real pizzazz. The city had just hosted the 1967 World's Fair, known as Expo '67. It was a leading candidate to host the Summer Olympic Games at the time; indeed, it would win the International Olympics Committee vote the next year and be named the venue for the 1976 Olympics.

The addition of the four new teams was the impetus for the creation of divisions in baseball. Each league, now composed of twelve teams rather than the traditional eight, was divided into two six-team divisions. The Expos were placed in the newly formed NL East. The new owners of the Montreal team, with a major league franchise suddenly dropped in their lap, had other concerns: where was the team going to play, and what are we going to call them?

The answer to the first question was Jarry Park, a wooden minor league park that seated 3,000. The owners supervised a frantic and shoddy makeover of the tiny park to build the capacity to 28,500, still the smallest in baseball.

As for the name, the obvious favorite was the Royals, as a nod to Montreal's baseball past. That name had unfortunately already been claimed by the brand-new Kansas City expansion team. The "Voyageurs" was briefly considered as an homage to Montreal's French history. The final winner: "Expos," after the 1967 Exposition held two years before.

One of the last names to be discarded for the new team? The "Montreal Nationals."

If you think that's an eerie coincidence, hang in there. It's going to get weirder.

The inaugural version of the Expos did what expansion teams are expected to do. They lost. A lot: 110 games.

By the second season, they had dramatically improved, going 73-89, then 71-90, escaping the NL East cellar for the first time. The Expos were still lingering below .500, but their scouts knew what they were doing. The Expos' farm system was filling up with top prospects. They signed a star high school quarterback from California named Gary Carter, and a superb high school athlete with bad knees named Andre Dawson. They found a juco outfielder by the name of Warren Cromartie, who had been drafted four times already, and turned them all down – but this time, the Expos convinced him to sign. They added an undrafted slugging third baseman, Larry Parrish, and a toolsy 17-year-old with a cannon for an arm, Ellis Valentine. And a college pitcher from Oklahoma named Steve Rogers.

Other things were improving for the team as well. In 1977, the Expos had moved from Jarry Park to the newly completed Olympic Stadium, built to host the track and field events for the 1976 Summer Olympics. By 1979, the Expos' eleventh season, the Expos were a joke no more. They were competing for the NL East title. Gary Carter was the best catcher in baseball, a cannon-armed receiver with a power bat. Dawson had won the 1977 Rookie of the Year award and was arguably the best all-around centerfielder in baseball, hitting 25 homers and stealing 35 bases. Parrish manned the hot corner with a .307 average and 30 home runs. Cromartie and Valentine ably patrolled the corner outfield slots.

Meanwhile, Steve Rogers was becoming one of the best pitchers in the National League. In 1977 he won 17 games, with 17 complete games (backed by the Expos' anemic run-scoring, he also lost 16). In '78, he went 13-10 with a 2.47 ERA, second-best in the NL. In '79, he led the league with five shutouts. In 1980, he went 16-11 with a 2.98 ERA, pitching 14 complete games. (Max Scherzer has 8 complete games– *in his life*.)

Olympic Stadium, the Nationals' second home. The Expos played here from 1977 until the move to Washington. The Blue Jays have begun a tradition of playing their final spring training games here. (*Photo credit: V.G. Bledsoe.*)

At this writing, Steve Rogers is the franchise leader for the Washington Nationals in the following categories: wins; strikeouts; games started; complete games; innings pitched; and shutouts. His franchise records for complete games and shutouts will never be eclipsed – no one will ever come close. Rogers has 37 career shutouts, all as an Expo. Of current Nats, second place goes to Max Scherzer with 4; after nine seasons, Stephen Strasburg has 2. Ditto for Rogers's 129 complete games: Scherzer has 7 as a Nat. Rogers has 158 franchise wins. Strasburg, when healthy, averages 13 wins a season. At that pace, barring injury, trade or retirement, he might overtake Rogers for the franchise lead in wins in 2023 – maybe.

In 1979, the new-look Expos, with Rogers as their ace, finished two measly games out of first. The next season was even more frustrating – they lost the division to the Phillies by a single game.

Then, in 1981, the unthinkable happened. On June 12, 55 games into the season, major league baseball players went on strike. For eight weeks, there was no baseball. When the labor issue was settled in late July, the owners had no idea how to resolve the pennant races. Roughly a third of the season had been wiped out by the strike. Did the teams simply pick up where they had left off? This would penalize the teams that had been behind at the beginning of the strike: they had lost fifty valuable and irreplaceable games they could have used to make up ground. The quirky compromise was to divide the season into two halves, pre-strike and post-strike, and let the division winners of each half play in a best-of-five series. Thus was born the very first "Division Series."

The Philadelphia Phillies had won the first half of the NL East race, and therefore were already in the playoffs. With a second season of 53 games to play, it was going to be a knife fight to win a chance to face the Phillies. It was Steve Rogers who put the Expos on his back. In that 53-game second half, he made nine starts, in which he pitched to a 1.96 ERA, holding opposing batters to a .196 batting average. The Expos went 30-23 post-strike and won the NL East – well, at least half of it – for the first time ever.[12]

Montreal was on to the best of five against the Phillies for the NL East championship. Unlike today's leisurely playoffs, designed for maximum television exposure, every game was to be played back-to-back, just like the regular season. Rogers of course got the ball in Game 1 to face the Phillies' Steve Carlton, the previous season's Cy Young winner. Rogers craftily scattered ten hits over 8 2/3 innings, yielding only one run before Jeff Reardon entered for a one-out save. The Expos went on to win the second game as well, 3-1, behind Bill Gullickson.

But the Phillies won Games 3 and 4, and it was back to Rogers v. Carlton once again. Carlton is in the Hall of Fame, and he was at the height of his prowess. In 1980, the previous year, he had gone 24-9,

---

12. The hard-luck Cardinals actually won the most games for the year in the division, but by finishing second in both halves, had to watch the Phillies and Expos fight it out for the NL East championship.

leading the league in wins, innings, and strikeouts. In the strike-shortened season of 1981, he had put up a 13-4 record with a 2.42 ERA. The man has four Cy Young awards.

But head to head, it was Rogers's day. He pitched a complete game, six-hit shutout. Not to be denied, he even drove in two runs off of Carlton, and *Les Expos* were NL East Champions.

On the other side of the bracket, the Los Angeles Dodgers had beaten the Astros to win the NL West playoff. In the five-game championship series, the teams would play the first two in Los Angeles, the remainder in Montreal. After his nine inning effort in the clincher against Philly, there was no possibility of Rogers starting Game 1 against LA; he'd have to wait until Game 3.

The teams split the first two games in Los Angeles. What did Rogers do in Game 3? He merely went out and pitched *another* complete game. Seven hits, five strikeouts, and a single earned run. Meanwhile, the Expos' Jerry White hit a three-run tater to pace them to a 4-1 victory.

At this point, Steve Rogers is simply unstoppable. His playoff line is 3-0, with a microscopic ERA of 0.68.

On the brink of elimination, the Dodgers responded in Game 4 with a 7-1 blowout. The rout was led by a 3 hit, 3 RBI game by......Dodgers left fielder and future Nats skipper, Dusty Baker.

Game 4 was played on a Saturday in near freezing temperatures. It's *Canada*. In *October*. Game Five was scheduled for the next day, Sunday. The weather forecast was for heavy rain and likely sleet or snow. Olympic Stadium was open to the elements (its long-promised roof would not arrive until the next year). Therefore, the league deemed it wise to postpone Game 5 until Monday.

It's known as Blue Monday to this day.

The Dodgers would start their incredible rookie pitcher, Fernando Valenzuela, the chubby screwballer from Mexico. With a 13-7 record in that shortened season, Valenzuela would win both the NL Rookie of the Year and Cy Young, having led the league in strikeouts and pitching 11 complete games. The Expos countered with Ray Burris, who had pitched a complete game shutout himself to win Game 2 of the series.

The Expos drew first blood when Tim Raines led off the bottom of the first with a double, and Rodney Scott, trying to sacrifice Raines over, was safe when the Dodgers tried to get Raines going to third. Both were safe. Andre Dawson hit into a double play, but Raines scored from third. 1-0, Expos.

Then, Burris and Valenzuela would throw up matching zeroes on the scoreboard inning after inning. Finally, in the top of the fifth, Burris surrendered a single to the Dodgers' Rick Monday. Another single advanced Monday to third, and he dashed home on a groundout by Valenzuela. Tie game, 1-1.

In the bottom of the fifth, Valenzuela retired the Expos in order. Burris did the same in the top of the sixth. Now it was Valenzuela's turn. 1-2-3. Now Burris, 1-2-3.

After eight innings, each pitcher has pitched a lights-out start. Valenzuela has given up three hits, Burris, five; each has surrendered a single run. In the top of the ninth, the Dodgers have the heart of the order coming up: Garvey, Cey, and Monday.

In the eighth, Expos skipper Jim Fanning had sent Rogers to the bullpen to warmup. Even though he had pitched a complete game three days earlier, Fanning believed that the red-hot Rogers gives them the best chance to win. Who could blame him? Rogers is undefeated in the playoffs. He has pitched, and won, three consecutive complete games in the playoffs (okay – he only went 8 2/3 in one – sue me) in which he has surrendered a total of two runs. Instead of going to closer Jeff Reardon, Fanning sent out Rogers to start the ninth.

Rogers's job is simple. It's a 1-1 game. He is to go out and shut down the Dodgers, as he has all series, until the Expos can score one run and win the game. Rogers threw one pitch to cleanup hitter Steve Garvey. He popped it up. One out. Then to Cey, he made a mistake. His trademark sinker didn't sink. Cey hit a towering fly to left. But the Penguin's shot died in the frigid Quebec air. Tim Raines camped out under it on the warning track, and there were two outs.

The next batter was Rick Monday. On a 3-1 count, Gary Carter called for another sinker. Again, Rogers hung it. Monday crushed it to centerfield.

The centerfield fence is 400 feet in Olympic Stadium. Andre Dawson drifted back, back, back, then reached the wall and watched in despair as Monday's shot easily cleared the fence.

Just like that, the Dodgers had won the game. In the ninth, Valenzuela recorded two outs in the ninth, but then walked Carter, then Parrish. On came Bob Welch, who got the save on a Jerry White groundout to second.

To this day, in Montreal, everyone knows it as Blue Monday. It is the single defining moment of agony for the franchise. Steve Rogers is their Bill Buckner. Not only did it happen on the first year that the Expos made the playoffs, *but the Montreal Expos would never make the playoffs again.*

Blue Monday's home, the Olympic Stadium interior. The picture is taken from deep right-center towards home plate. (There is no outfield fence in place. The stadium was being set up for a monster truck rally.) There would have been no roof at the time of Blue Monday. (*Photo credit: V.G. Bledsoe.*)

Olympic Stadium, first base side. (*Photo credit: V.G. Bledsoe.*)

Let's sum this up.

On Monday, October 19, 1981, the Montreal Expos, in a must-win final Game 5, in the NL Championship Series, decided to use their red-hot, ace starter, on short rest, as a reliever, rather than their bullpen. He recorded two outs, then disaster struck. The Expos lose the game and thus the series.

Thirty-six years later, on Thursday, October 12, 2017, the same franchise, now called the Washington Nationals, in a must-win final Game 5, in the NL Division Series, decided to use their red-hot, ace starter, on short rest, as a reliever, rather than their bullpen. He recorded two outs, then disaster struck. The Nationals lose the game and thus the series.

Blue Monday; Black Thursday. Steve Rogers; Max Scherzer. The Curse of the Nationals is the Curse of the Expos, merely extended. It is clear to get to the bottom of the Curse of the Nationals, we are going to need to look beyond the 2005 start of the Washington franchise.

So we will start where in all began – in Canada.

CHAPTER 5

Curses (Foiled Again)

WE'VE ALREADY DOCUMENTED THE UNBELIEVABLE annual tragedies that the Nats have endured. We've seen the eerie specter of Blue Monday, which was repeated, almost blow for blow, thirty-six years later in Max Scherzer's Chernobylesque meltdown. To those still not accepting the reality of this curse, and its genesis with the team in its Montreal version, consider the rest of the Expos' accursed history.

From 1979 to 1983, the Expos won more games than any other National League team. Yet that success yielded them one, and only one, trip to the playoffs: the Blue Monday playoffs. (If this seems familiar, yes, it smacks of a later version of the Expos: the 2012-2017 Nationals, who won an average of 92 games a season in that timespan, with nothing to show for it.)

After 1983 came a decade of mediocrity for Montreal. Unfortunately, they were in the same division as the New York Mets and the St. Louis Cardinals, who were both in their heydays. The 1986 Expos went 78-83 – not great, but within shouting distance of a .500 record. They finished the season almost 30 games behind the Mets, who went on to win the World Series against the Billy Buckner Red Sox.

Until 1994.

In 1994, Montreal lost 9 of their first 13 games. Then, 8 ½ games out of first, something clicked. They won 11 out of their next 12 to close within a half game of first-place. In mid-July, they grabbed it for good. Led by an incredible home-grown outfield of Larry Walker (.322, 44 doubles), Marquis Grissom (.288, 36 steals), and Moises Alou (.339, 22 homers), they had built a seven-game lead over the powerhouse Atlanta Braves by August 10 – the Greg Maddux, Tom Glavine, and John Smoltz Braves, who had rattled off three straight division wins. No Montreal team had ever won more than 95 games in a season. This one was on pace to win 105.

Except that they were cursed.

On August 11, the Major League Baseball Players Association announced that the players were going on strike – again. While the players representatives and owners would negotiate on and off for the next month (President Clinton even summoned them to the White House for an afternoon in an attempt to mediate the dispute), both sides were sticking to their guns. The labor dispute would not be resolved until the spring of the next year.

Since 1903, except for a single year, 1904, when the National League snobbishly boycotted, there had always been a World Series. The Series was the annual fall ritual that symbolized America, and captivated the attention of its citizens. It had not been cancelled for World War I, nor for the Great Depression, nor for World War II. Now, for the first time in almost a century, there would be no postseason play. The first-place Expos, who had been cruising to the playoffs, would have no chance to redeem Blue Monday. Tantalus had awakened again.

The strike was resolved in April 1995, but the Expos would never again compete for a playoff berth. Strapped for cash even before the strike, the Expos had to deal off star after star. They lost Larry Walker to free agency. Marquis Grissom was traded to the Braves. Ken Hill and his 16-5 record went to the Cards. The team that had been on pace to win 105 games in 1994 would, one year later, finish dead last in the division, 24 games out of first.

A decade of failure, occasionally relieved by mere mediocrity, ensued. Crowds dwindled: the Expos routinely played home games before crowds of two or three thousand spectators. In the ten years after the disastrous *baseballus interruptus* in 1994, the Expos finished last in the NL East three times, and next to last five times.

The franchise simply could not be sustained on a financial level. While the team took in its revenues in Canadian dollars, it had to pay its baseball salaries in American greenbacks. In the early 1990s, the Canadian dollar was worth about 85 cents in US dollars. By 1999, it had dropped to less than 65 American cents.

Furthermore, Olympic Stadium was easily the most unappealing venue in the sport. Designed as a track and field/all-purpose venue, it had never been a good fit for baseball. The roof had lain dormant in a French warehouse for years, not arriving until 1982. The outfield astroturf had been installed in sections, and now the sections weren't level with each other, creating hazardous seams more than an inch high where the sections met. Imagine playing in an outfield with random curbs running through it. The stadium was literally falling apart: a 55-ton chunk of the roof dropped to the ground in 2002 before a game against the Padres.

A new baseball-only stadium was needed to attract fans. The owners couldn't afford it, and the government of Montreal, still trying to pay off the scandalously exorbitant bill for hosting the Olympics, wasn't in any position to help. Quebecers referred to the Olympic Stadium as the "Big Owe," as its actual construction costs had almost doubled the projected budget.[13] Not surprisingly, there was zero political or public support for another stadium.

But perhaps the most grievous blow to the Expos had come in 1977, when baseball decided to add another team in Canada. At the time, the Expos' ownership had enthusiastically endorsed the creation of another Canadian professional baseball team, but it could have not known the monster it was creating a mere 300 miles away. Toronto had eclipsed Montreal as the cultural and financial capital of Canada, and it was awarded a new franchise called the Blue Jays. Unlike Montreal, the Blue Jays had no trouble filling their stadium. Their team was good. While

---

13. The public debt for Olympic Stadium would not be paid off until 2006 – thirty years after its construction, and a year after the Expos left for Washington.

Montreal put up so-so records from 1985–1993, the Jays won five division championships in that span. They won back-to-back World Series in 1992 and 1993. Inevitably, little by little, Expos fans slipped away to root for the Blue Jays.

The outcome? While the Expos had developed a scouting and drafting system that was the envy of baseball, they couldn't afford to pay the stars that their system produced. Their players were affordable only while they were under team control, roughly six years in the majors. When those players became eligible for free agency, the franchise could never hope to match the salary offers of the rest of the league for the services of their talented stars. That the Expos had unearthed and developed those stars made it all the more unbearable.

So dismal offseason after dismal offseason, the fans of the team watched their superstars be traded, or simply walk away in free agency. The face of the franchise, Gary Carter, became a Met after the '84 season. Then Andre Dawson left for free agency after the '86 season. Then Tim Raines after 1990, Andres Galarraga after '91, Tim Wallach after '92, Dennis Martinez after '93, and Larry Walker after '94. John Wetteland became a Yankee, and Pedro Martinez went to Boston.

The fanbase dropped to next to nothing. They could hardly be blamed, having watched their favorite players saunter off to happier places winter after winter. Attendance fell. In 1983, the Expos had watched 2.3 million fans walk through the turnstiles at Olympic Stadium. In 2001, only 642,745 fans bothered to show up – an untenable decline of 75 percent. On September 19, 2001, the Expos played the Marlins before a paid attendance of 2,887 fans. In 2002, in late April, they played before 3,501 – while they were in first place.

When Jeffrey Loria became the Expos' managing general partner and tried to get a new TV deal to broadcast the games for the 2000 season, TNS, the Canadian national sports station, offered them $5,000 per game for the broadcast rights. TNS had been paying the Blue Jays $200,000 a game. A local Montreal radio station offered to broadcast the games – but only if it didn't have to pay for the rights. Insulted, the Expos broadcast the games themselves – on the internet.

The Expos, unloved and unwatched, were becoming an embarrassment, the red-headed stepchild of baseball. Now there began serious discussions of contraction – reducing the number of major league baseball teams by culling the weakest franchises – driven mostly by a desire of putting the Expos out of baseball's collective misery. In 2001, it happened. Contraction was approved by the MLB owners by a 30-2 vote. Baseball would reduce each league by a single team. The Twins drew the short straw in the AL. There was no doubt who was going to be kicked out of the National League.

While the Twins would fight tooth and nail and survive, baseball in Montreal appeared to be dead. However, along came a deal. It was bizarre and it was incestuous, but it saved the Expos from disappearing into the void. In 2002, John Henry, then the owner of the Florida Marlins, bid on and was awarded the Boston Red Sox. Jeffrey Loria, the owner of the Expos, then traded the Expos for the Marlins, leaving the Expos ownerless. They became the foster child of MLB: a team owned and operated by Major League Baseball itself.

The act of having MLB take a team into stewardship was unprecedented. It made no sense: the Expos were now collectively owned by the other teams, who each owned one-twenty-ninth of the franchise. That's right – the Expos were now owned by their opponents.

The whole thing stunk. The conflicts of interest were systemic and unavoidable. Here was a baseball team that was owned by, and funded by, the other 29 teams. How could the Expos make equitable trades with the other teams who owned them? The Expos' opponents would collectively dictate how much money the Expos could spend on player salaries – how could that possibly work? The deal may have temporarily saved the Montreal franchise, but it gave the appearance that the Expos were being maintained as baseball's equivalent of the Washington Generals, the never-victorious opponents in the Harlem Globetrotters' make-believe games, a dummy team for the rest of the league to beat up on.

Still, no one was really sure what was going to happen to the 'Spos. Contraction was still a quite real possibility. Meanwhile, fans "stayed away in droves," as the old saying goes. The final insult? In 2003, MLB decided to take a quarter of the Expos home games and play them in Puerto Rico. Slowly, the talk of contraction dwindled. But what to do with the Expos?

To the rescue came a city without baseball. Washington was no longer the town that had failed to support two Senators teams. It was far and away the largest metropolitan area without a baseball team in the United States. Baseball had expanded three times since the second version of the Senators left for greener pastures in Texas, but had refused to put another team in Washington.[14] When even the Tampa Bay area got a team in 1998, it was risibly obvious that the DC area was being passed over for a single and not very good reason: namely, to avoid arousing the ire of the Baltimore Orioles and their litigious owner, asbestos trial lawyer Peter Angelos.[15] While the Senators had supported the move of the St. Louis Browns in 1953 to become the Orioles, Angelos had made it clear that he had no intention of returning the favor to allow a new team in Washington, just over thirty miles away from Camden Yards.

Now in 2005, over the Orioles' objection, MLB decided that the Expos were coming to Washington. There were three and a half million potential fans in the D.C. metro area, far too many to continue to ignore. The D.C. government had promised to build a state of the art stadium in the District. And MLB was dying to unload the ugly stepchild.

And so the French-Canadian Expos became the Nationals of the American capital. And brought with them their curse.

Still not convinced?

How about this? There were three other teams created the same year as the Expo/Nats – the Padres, the Brewers, and the Royals. Every single one has won a pennant; between them, they account for seven league championships and two World Series championships. The Padres won a pennant in their 16th year of existence. The Brewers took 14 years to

---

14. The Padres were in talks to move from San Diego to replace the second-time Senators in the mid-1970s, but it never came to fruition.

15. And litigious he is. Angelos viewed the DC area and its fans as the Orioles' rightful property. The Nationals and Orioles are still as of this writing fighting over the division of TV revenues, almost fifteen years after the Expos became the Nats.

win their pennant, and the Royals only 11. Only the Nationals are still virgins.

How about this? There have been six teams created <u>after</u> the Nationals in 1969. Among them, they have accumulated seven pennants and five world championships. The Marlins won the whole ball of wax in their fifth year of existence. They won it again six years later. The Diamondbacks won the World Series in their fourth year of existence.

How about this? There are only two teams in baseball that have never won a pennant. (The Mariners, born eight years later, are the other one.)

When, yet again, the Nationals didn't win the pennant in 2018, they held the honor of never winning their league at any time in their first fifty years of existence. No other team in baseball has ever gone as long from its founding without ever once winning a pennant. The Texas Rangers came close. The Rangers (who used to be the Washington Senators, let us not forget) finally won a pennant in 2010, their 50th season exactly. When the Nats don't win the National League again in 2019, it will be the fifty-first season of failure, extending their all-time record.

None of the famous cursed teams has ever had, at any time in its existence, a fifty-year stretch without winning a pennant. The Red Sox's longest stretch without a pennant was only 27 seasons, 1919 through 1945. The Cubbies? Thirty-eight seasons (1946 through 1983). The Indians suffered through a 40-year dry spell. The Expos/Nationals have them all beat by a decade - so far. The White Sox hold second place with 45 consecutive pennantless seasons, a streak of futility that ended in 2005. Every year, the Nats continue to pad their shameful lead.

If you're still not convinced, consider this. The Nats could claim to be the most feckless club not just in baseball, but in any of the four major sports of baseball, football, basketball, and hockey. The Nationals hold the longest streak for any team in any of the four major sports to have never made it to the championship game of their sport since their creation. In other words, no other major professional sports team, in any league, has ever failed to make it to its championship series for the first 50 years of its existence. The Buffalo Braves/Los Angeles Clippers are in second place; like the Nats, they've never made the championship finals at any time in their history. But they're also eighteen months younger than the Nats – their initial season was 1970-71.

But what did the Expos do to offend the baseball gods?

Did the owner of the Expos trade away a godlike player like Ruth? Or, barring that, perhaps a demigod (?) hero like, say, Rocky Colavito?

Had, decades ago, some Expo fan been barred from bringing his prize hog into Jarry Park, and stormed off, his echoing words a poignant malediction upon the team and all its descendants?

Had some fast food restaurant mascot been wrongfully thrown into the St. Lawrence River? Or some other unforgivable act of impiety?

In order to lift the Curse, first we must discover the source of the Curse. There are no detective agencies specializing in baseball curse tracing. It's up to us. So curse-hunting we will go.

CHAPTER 6

In Search of Babe Ruth, or Barring That, Rocky Colavito

So we've established that the Nationals are cursed, and that the Curse stems, not from the time that they were Nationals, but going back all the way to the time that they were the Expos. We also know that the Curse was in existence at least before Blue Monday in October 1981. So we can eliminate any possible origin story that postdates that disastrous day.

In our role as curse detectives, our first suspect must be, like the Red Sox and the Indians, the Greek Tragedy Trade, where a beloved team player is traded away. Trading Babe Ruth for a Broadway musical is the Platonic ideal of such a trade – they literally traded him for a song (or songs). Did the Expos have one?

It bears repeating. There is only one Babe Ruth. He is simply the greatest baseball player who ever lived. And he did it all powered by hot dogs, oysters, and beer, not performance-enhancing hormones.

If you're a Ty Cobb advocate, or a Willie Mays advocate, or like me, a Hank Aaron fan, you're really arguing about second place. It would take pages to list the career records that Babe Ruth set that still stand untouched today. But even those records do not do justice to the phenomenon of the Babe. During the early 1910s, there was a player, John Franklin Baker, whose power was so incredible and so well known that everyone knew him by his nickname: Home Run Baker. From 1911 to 1914 he led the American League each year in home runs. His season high was in 1913, when he hit the unbelievable, astronomical total of….. twelve.

Six years later, in his first year of full time play as a position player, the Babe hit 29 home runs. He also went 9-5 in 15 starts as a pitcher. With the exception of 1925, that would be the fewest home runs he would hit for the next 14 seasons. In 1920, his first year as a Yankee, he hit 54; the entire Red Sox team that had just traded him had only 22.

He is the all-time career leader in slugging percentage at .6897. That doesn't include the over 2000 times in his career the opposing team walked him rather than let him hit.

On top of that, he was probably the best *pitcher* of the 1910s. He didn't become a full time outfielder until his last year with the Red Sox, 1919. That means by pitching from 1915-18, he was deprived of about 1500 at-bats, which likely robbed him of the opportunity to hit another 75-100 homers, maybe more. Add those to his 714, and his home record would likely be still intact and safely out of reach of anyone.

So who's the Expos' version of Babe Ruth?

To explain that, we're going to need to delve into modern statistical analysis. As long as baseball has been played, there has been disagreement over what is more valuable: offense (hitting, getting walks, basestealing, making "productive outs") or defense (fielding, throwing, but mostly pitching.) There's been even greater disagreement perhaps in comparing position players to each other. Who's more valuable: Babe Ruth, a slugger without peer but a middling glove in the outfield, or Willie Mays, a great hitter and a superb defensive centerfielder? A dazzling shortstop like Ozzie Smith, whose range and arm prevent runs every game, or a slugger like Willie McCovey, who plays first where the effect of his iron glove is minimized? Lou Gehrig, who played on Yankees teams surrounded by stars, or Ernie Banks, who played his entire career on terrible Cubs teams? Who's more valuable, a pitcher like Max Scherzer, or a hitter like Bryce Harper?

In comparing players from different decades, how do you account for sea changes in the game, like changes to the equipment, changes to stadiums' sizes, changes to the rules, changes to pitching philosophy, changes to managers' strategies? Or how about changes to who is allowed to play the game, as when baseball was finally integrated in the

1940s? All of these clearly affect the statistics that are being recorded. But how much? How to quantify that difference?

Baseball geeks have struggled to find a statistical philosopher's stone, a single statistic that would allow all aspects of the game – hitting, fielding, pitching, baserunning – to be compared in a scientific and equitable way. These geeks, who call themselves sabermetricians,[16] believe they accomplished that with the statistic of Wins Above Replacement, or "WAR."

WAR builds on a concept started by the patron saint of sabermetricians, Bill James. He created "the replacement player," an agreed fictional standard of the stats that a hypothetical substitute baseball player – the guy waiting in the wings to be called up from the minor leagues – would accomplish in a full season. The stat of Wins Above Replacement is supposed, through arcane formulas, some esoteric stat-crunching, and more than a little outright guesswork, to give an approximate value for how much better or worse Player X is than that hypothetical replacement player. The value is expressed in "Wins Above Replacement." It's the measure of how many extra wins in a season, or a career, that Player X would create for his team, by his actions on the field, than the hypothetical replacement player would.[17]

For example, Max Scherzer's Cy Young season in 2017 clocked in at 7.1 Wins Above Replacement. That statistic means that due to his efforts on the field, the Nationals won around seven more games than they would have if, instead of Max, they had called up their best pitcher from their AAA club. With Max, the Nats went 97-65. Without Max (hypothetically) they only go 90-72.

But the true genius of WAR is its attempt to account for, and give a value for, everything a player does in a game, good or bad, in terms of how it contributes to the winning of a baseball game. And, the statheads

---

16. Metric as in measuring, and "saber" as a nod to SABR, the Society of American Baseball Research, their geek club, if you will.
17. It's also possible to have a negative WAR over the course of a season, which means that the player performed worse than a top minor leaguer.

believe, WAR accounts for differences in what position a player plays, what era the player plays in, or how crappy his teammates are. Thus, they claim, WAR allows the accurate head-to-head comparison of pitchers to batters, of shortstops to first basemen, or players from the 1920s to players from the 2010s. And the stat is cumulative: each season of WAR is added to the next, to arrive at a career WAR.[18]

Babe Ruth is the all-time leader in career WAR, with 183.7.

So if the Expos have to come up with the equivalent of Babe Ruth for their Curse, it can't be done.

But Rocky Colavito? Sure, we can do that. Easily. The tragic parade of Expos stars out the door is long and, well, tragic.

How about...Gary Carter? Carter was an eleven-time All-Star. He's the best defensive catcher ever in the history of the game not named Ivan Rodriguez. He racked up a career WAR of 69.9. Of that, 55.6 WAR were earned as an Expo, making Gary the Nationals franchise leader in career WAR. Gary went to the Mets before the 1985 season.

Or Andre Dawson? Either he or the Braves' Dale Murphy was the best all-around centerfielder of his era. Dawson was NL Rookie of the Year in 1977, as well as league MVP with the Cubs in 1987. Eight Gold Gloves. 438 career home runs. 1591 runs batted in. His career sadly hampered at the end by years of injuries to knees damaged in high school, the Hawk still accumulated a career WAR of 64.5. He's a Hall of Famer (and went in as an Expo). He was allowed to walk away after 1986 season, one year after Carter.

Or how about Tim Raines? Another Hall of Famer who also went in wearing an Expos cap. A 7-time All-Star who stole 70 bases or more six seasons, including a 90-steal season in 1983. Lifetime .294 hitter. WAR: 69.1. Traded after 1990 season.

---

18. Like all religions, sabermetrics has its schisms. There are actually 2 widely used but slightly varying WAR configurations: one known as "bWAR," calculated by the folks at Baseball-Reference, and the other known as "fWAR," calculated by the folks at Fangraphs. The statistics quoted herein, for the nerds, are all bWAR.

Dennis Martinez: 245 wins. More than Juan Marichal, Whitey Ford, or Jim Bunning, all of whom are in Cooperstown. Career WAR 49.5. Became a free agent after 1993 season.

Larry Walker. Maybe the best player who ever played who is not in Cooperstown who is eligible for induction. A fantastic defensive outfielder, and he was a Canadian to boot! Career stats: .313, OPS .966. Career WAR of 72.6. Became a free agent in October 1994.

Vladimir Guerrero. A first ballot Hall of Famer, inducted in the class of 2018. A free-swinging .318 lifetime batting average, with 449 career homeruns. AL league MVP. Career WAR 59.3. Allowed to walk away after the 2003 season.

No? Wait, I got it. Pedro Martinez. You may have heard of him. Three Cy Young awards. Won five league ERA titles. In 1997, as an Expo, he went 17-8 with an unheard-of 1.90 ERA. In 2000, with Boston, pitching in one of the best hitter's parks in baseball, he topped it: 18-6 with a 1.74 ERA. Finished his career with a WAR of 86, placing him among the 20 greatest pitchers in the history of baseball. The Expos traded him after his 1997 season.

With no offense intended to Indians fans, every single one of these guys was better than Rocky Colavito – a lot better. Rocky's ended his career with a respectable 44.5 WAR. Every single one of the Expos' prodigal sons is better. So if trading Rocky was enough to put a hex on the Indians, any one of these Expos would be more than sufficient for the Curse of the Nats.

There was another guy who was much, much better than Rocky Colavito. He was a September callup for the Expos in 1988. He started only four games, but went 3-0 with a 2.42 ERA. Then he was traded in a package to Seattle for Mark Langston. After that 3-0 start with the Expos, he pitched another two decades. He did all right. His accomplishments:

- Most strikeouts per 9 innings, 10.6
- Five Cy Youngs, including four in a row – 1999-2002
- Four ERA titles
- Five seasons with 300 Ks, including a 372-K season

- 303 career wins
- 4,875 career strikeouts, second only to Nolan Ryan
- By WAR, the ninth best pitcher in the history of baseball: 104.3

Yep, that is Hall of Famer Randy Johnson.

Nobody is Babe Ruth. But Randy Johnson is, according to career WAR, worth two and a half Rocky Colavitos. And if Rocky can cause a curse, so then, *a fortiori,* can the Big Unit. And there we have it. Mystery solved: the Curse of Randy Johnson.

There's only one problem with the theory. Each one of these Expos left the team <u>after</u> Blue Monday: Carter was the first to go, three years after the 1981 disaster, Vlad the last after the 2003 season. Since we know the Curse was in place in 1981, we need a Colavito who was traded <u>before</u> Blue Monday. Sorry, but Randy Johnson was traded in 1989, after Blue Monday by years.

We have to keep looking.

CHAPTER 7

The Curse of Le Grand Orange

THERE ARE ONLY FIVE RETIRED numbers in the Washington Nationals organization. One is 42, belonging to Jackie Robinson, when baseball ordered every team to retire it in honor of Robinson's breaking baseball's color barrier.

Of the remaining four, three are people we've already discussed, and eliminated: Gary Carter, Andre Dawson, and Tim Raines.

Andre Dawson's No. 10 was retired twice: once for Dawson, and once for Montreal's very first superstar: Rusty Staub.

Now, maybe, we're getting somewhere.

In 1962, the brand-new Houston Colt .45s signed a high school star from New Orleans named Daniel Joseph Staub, known from birth as Rusty for his red hair. In 1963, after an impressive single year in the minors, Rusty was called up by Houston and thrust into its opening day lineup less than ten days after his 19th birthday. While most teams would let such a prospect season for several more years in the minor leagues, the new Houston franchise had no such luxury. They had spent the then-enormous sum of $90,000 on Staub's signing bonus. They wanted an immediate payoff.

When Rusty struggled in his first season in 1963, Houston seemed to sour on him. He was even sent down to the minors in the middle of the 1964 season. After a while, the feeling was mutual. Even after he blossomed into one of the league's best hitters (hitting .333 in pitching-dominant 1967), Astros management seemed unhappy with their red-headed right fielder.

The winter before the Expos' first season, in order to give the new franchises an initial core of experienced players, MLB held an expansion draft. Each current MLB team was allowed to place 15 of its players off-limits. The new expansion teams were allowed to draft any of the remaining unprotected players. After the other teams had posted their lists of protected players, what was left in the draft pool were mostly veterans past their prime and younger, unproven players.

The Expos' draft strategy emphasized taking well-known, if declining, veterans. Their hope was to assemble a body of established "name" players that 1) their new fans would recognize, and 2) they might be able to dangle in front of other clubs to extract prospects in a trade.

Two of such "name" players the Expos seized upon were Jesus Alou, the Stephen Baldwin of the three Alou brothers, and Donn Clendenon, a decent starting first baseman for the Pirates. Quickly after drafting them, Montreal was able to convince Houston (now called the Astros, after the burgeoning space program based there) to take Alou and Clendenon in exchange for Rusty Staub. The Expos were ecstatic with the trade. So apparently was Staub.

Only one problem: Clendenon refused to report to Houston, saying he would prefer to retire and get a real job rather than play for the Astros.

But the Expos were desperate to keep Staub. He had reported to the Expos' camp for spring training. The Astros, understandably, said it was Clendenon or nothing – the deal was off. The Expos were undaunted. They quickly stuck Staub in an Expos uniform and proceeded to have a photographer snap roll after roll of Rusty Staub the Expo, including one with the brand-new Commissioner of Baseball, Bowie Kuhn. The effect of the photo op ambush was that Kuhn was seen as "blessing" the trade, and the Astros had to back down. The Expos convinced Houston to take pitcher Jack Billingham and some greenbacks instead.[19]

---

19. They even convinced Clendenon to unretire and play for the Expos; they would trade him midseason to the Mets. The Mets would win the 1969 Series, where Clendenon would hit .357 and three home runs and be named Series MVP.

The Expos, though, got what they wanted. Delighted to be with a franchise that actually wanted him, Staub would continue his ascension into becoming one of the best players in the game. In 1969, his first year in Montreal, he would hit .302 with 29 home runs. He would slug .529 that year, with an on-base percentage of .426, both career bests. His OPS, .952, was fourth best in the National League. In 1970, his average dropped to .274, but he still hit 30 home runs. In 1971, he played all 162 games, hitting .311 and driving in 97 runs.

A deeper dive into the stats yields even more fruit. Staub's outstanding batting eye yielded walks: 110 in 1969 and 112 in 1970. Despite his ability to hit home runs, Staub prided himself on being first and foremost a contact hitter, a skill that would last for virtually his entire 23 year career. Those 110 bases on balls in 1969 were accompanied by only 61 strikeouts. In fact, he would from 1967 to 1983 – 17 consecutive seasons --never have more strikeouts than walks in a season. (By comparison, the Nats' Bryce Harper – one of the most frequently walked players in modern baseball – has never had a season where he had fewer strikeouts than walks.)

Staub was never completely satisfied with his hitting, showing up with a new batting stance on a regular basis. But despite his endless tinkering, the hitting never ceased. He led the Expos in WAR every year he was on the team. He is still second on the Nationals career leaderboard in OBP (.402 behind Nick Johnson's .408), and third in OPS (.899, trailing only Vlad Guerrero's ungodly .978 and Harper, by a single point).

In addition to his undeniable on-field achievements, his personality and efforts to win over the Montreal fans made him the face of the franchise. His flaming ginger hair and known eccentricities, such as carrying a full set of cookware on road trips to cook his own meals, were a good start to endearing himself to the fans. Staub wanted to not just be an Expo, but a proud citizen of Montreal. Dubbed by a local sportswriter, Ted Blackman, as *Le Grand Orange* ("Big Red"), Staub knew that being a Montrealer meant speaking French. He diligently began learning the language, informally at first, then with a tutor. Slowly, his fluency increased to the point where he felt comfortable being interviewed in

French. He could now explain how he managed a *coupe de circuite* (home run) off the *balle papillon* (knuckleball) the opposing *lanceur* (pitcher) had served up *en la manche troisieme* (third inning), or the *vol au sol* (shoestring catch) he made to save *le match*.

Maybe *Les Expos* had little chance of going to *la Series mondiale*, but there was no doubt that their ambassador of baseball to the French-speaking populace of Quebec was *Le Grand Orange*. Staub became a tireless promoter of the team. He traveled to backwater, French-only towns every winter to meet with small contingents of fans. To overcome the popularity of Canada's first love, hockey, he appeared on broadcasts of Canadiens games, and gave interviews, in both languages, about the summertime game also being played in Montreal. He was the head of the Young Expos Club, designed to attract the kids of Quebec and instill in them a love of baseball.

And then, it happened. The Expos traded Rusty Staub. Not only the best player on the team, but the most beloved player on the team. To the Mets, right before spring training started in 1972.

The package the Mets sent back was not inconsiderable. The Expos received outfielder Ken Singleton, shortstop Tim Foli, and first baseman Mike Jorgensen. All three were younger than Staub; all three were major league ready. And all three were cheaper than Staub, who was under contract to make the "exorbitant" salary of $90,000 that year for the Expos.

Singleton would put in three solid years as an Expo, hitting .302 in one season, before going off to star for the Baltimore Orioles as an OF/DH. Jorgensen, with good plate discipline but modest power, became the everyday Montreal first baseman; he would put up below average hitting numbers and excellent on-base numbers for five years in Montreal. He would manage to play another nine years for various teams in a 17-year career. Foli, a good field/no hit SS, would make up for his Punch-and-Judy bat with outstanding defensive play as the Expos shortstop for the next six years. He would vacuum up double play balls behind Steve Rogers' sinker, consistently rating as one of the most valuable defenders in the league.

What happened to Rusty?

He would go on to play for not only the Mets, but the Tigers, the Rangers, and the Mets again. He would gravitate to a DH/first baseman role, then become a pinch-hitting specialist. And he kept hitting. At age 39, as a New York Met, he hit .296 in a pinch-hitting role over 114 at-bats. He finished with 2,716 hits in his career. He is to this day the only major leaguer to have 500 hits for four different teams. Only four hitters have ever hit a home run both as a teenager and as a forty-year-old; Staub is one of them.

But as long as he played, and the incredible career numbers he put up, he never again hit like he did in Montreal. His lowest WAR for a season as an Expo was 5.9. Thereafter, his highest for teams other than Montreal were in 1975 and 1976, when he put up 2.9 in each. He played more seasons, more games, and had more plate appearances as a Met, a Tiger, and an Astro than as an Expo. Yet his WAR as an Expo is higher than for any other franchise: 18.5.

The Curse of *Le Grand Orange*? Well, it certainly seems like it.

Rusty put up a career WAR of 45.8. Thus, according to the sabermetricians, he had a better career – slightly – than Rocky Colavito (WAR of 44.5). In my book, he's significantly better. He's 13th all-time in games played, with 2,951. Cal Ripken, baseball's "Iron Man," has just 50 more. Rusty has more hits than Mickey Mantle. He has more hits than Ted Williams, more than Joe DiMaggio. If trading Rocky can doom the Indians for perpetuity, then trading Rusty can certainly do the same for the Expo-Nationals.

That's it. We found the source of the Curse. Trading Rusty, the face of the franchise, Mr. Expo, for a mess of potage. We're done with our sleuthing.

Except….Rusty came back. For one glorious half-season.

In 1979, the Montreal Expos came out of the gate rip-snorting. They went 14-5 in April, then 15-10 in May. By the end of June, they had a six- game lead in the NL East. But in July, they started to falter, and by mid-July the lead was down to a game and a half. They needed some help at the trade deadline to fix their offensive woes, and they knew just the man they needed. On July 20, 1979, the Detroit Tigers traded Rusty back to Montreal for minor leaguer Randall Schafer and cash.

Serge Touchette, the beat writer for *le Journal de Montreal*, described the scene of Rusty's first game back in Jonah Keri's *Up, Up, and Away*:

> They're playing Pittsburgh, eighth inning, down a run. The PA announcer didn't even get to say Rusty's name. As soon as he touched the on-deck circle, people went nuts. Chuck Tanner changed pitchers. And the whole time, Rusty is just standing there, waiting, and people were just losing their minds. This kept going and going for several minutes. It was the greatest ovation I'd ever heard in my life.

After the 5-minute ovation by 59,000 fans, Staub flied out to right.

Armed with Rusty's bat, the Expos' quest for the pennant continued. But the Pittsburgh Pirates had doggedly pursued the Expos, and in early August, they caught them, then passed them, building a four-game lead. The re-Rusty-fied Expos regained their fire. In August 28, they ripped off a ten-game winning streak, lost a game, then won 7 straight again: 17 out of 18. Unfortunately, there was another team that was just as hot – the Pirates. Then, on September 20, the Expos regained first place in the division by half a game. If they could hold off the Pirates for ten more games, they would have their first division championship. But they couldn't. The Expos went to Pittsburgh for a four game series, and took 3 out of 4, and the lead. For good. The Expos finished with 95 wins, second most in the league, but alas, also second most in their division. The "We are Family" Pirates would go on to win the World Series that year.

Rusty played just 38 games in his return to Montreal. But the prodigal son had returned, and the wrong had been righted, seven years later. That takes off the curse, right? That's how curses work.

Hold your horses, *mon ami*. On March 31, 1980, just days before Opening Day, the Expos traded Rusty AGAIN – to the Texas Rangers, this time for Chris Smith and LaRue Washington. Who? Exactly. [20]

How does the second Rusty Trade make sense? Well, the Expos liked their outfield, and it was impressive: Dawson in center, Ellis Valentine in right, and they had just picked up Ron Leflore to play left field. Rusty's best days as a defensive right fielder were well behind him. The only other possibility, first base, was occupied by Warren Cromartie. But the reality was that the Expos thought Rusty was done as a hitter. As we noted, since leaving eight years ago, he had never duplicated his early Montreal years. 1979 had seen a real dropoff in his production, as he hit only .244 in his split service with the Tigers and Expos.

The guys Montreal got in exchange? Smith had a total of nine at bats as an Expo and was out of baseball by 1984. The fabled LaRue Washington never played a single game as an Expo, and was out of baseball by 1982.

Meanwhile, the big redhead went to Texas, where he put up numbers for the Rangers, hitting .300 and slugging .459 in just over 100 games. Rusty wasn't done by a long shot. After the Rangers, he went on to play another five seasons for the Mets, hitting .276 there, mostly as a pinch-hitter.

Pinch-hitting is widely acknowledged as the most difficult job in baseball. The pinch-hitting specialist sits in the dugout, drinking coffee and shooting the breeze with his teammates for seven innings or so. Then, he walks out, cold, having sat on the bench for two hours, for a single at-bat against a pitcher throwing the ball more than 90 miles an hour.

Rusty is one of the best pinch-hitters in the history of the game. In 1983, at the age of 39, he made eight consecutive pinch hit appearances. He drilled eight consecutive hits. That same year, he had 25 RBIs as

---

20. Indians fans will tell you that they've been down this road, as Rocky Colavito endured the same indignity. The repentant Indians brought him back in 1965, then traded him again to the White Sox two years later. The Indians' hex remains, so clearly the act of bringing back the disrespected hero doesn't do squat if you then trade him again.

a pinch-hitter. Unbelievable: 25 RBI in 94 pinch-hit appearances. Give Rusty 500 at bats at that pace, and he'd have over 130 RBI – which would have led all of baseball that year. He finished the year with 132 plate appearances. He struck out just 10 times.

So the Expos traded this hero, not once, but twice. Heck, you could even argue that even the Red Sox only traded Babe Ruth once. Have we finally found the source of the Nationals Curse?

Baseball curses can be placed. They can also be lifted by the baseball gods under the proper circumstances, if the offenders are sufficiently remorseful and make proper acts of contrition. The Montreal Expos brought *Le Grand Orange* back in 1993 for a ceremony to have his number retired. That celebration is the sort of appropriate act of atonement that should lift the curse of Rusty Staub for good. The Red Sox never retired Babe Ruth's number. The Indians never retired Rocky Colavito's. Rusty's No. 10 was so honored, and with it, any bad mojo associated with trading Rusty (twice) would have been laid to rest. The slate is clean.

Rusty was so far our best candidate for the Nationals Curse. But he's not the cause. We have to keep looking. The search for the murderer of the Nats continues.

CHAPTER 8

The Curse of Pablo Escobar?

AS ANY TRUE FAN OF the Expos knows, Montreal is a party town. And there was never a party like there was in the early 1980s. It was the time of disco, and Montreal's disco scene was second only to New York's. Even as disco faded in the States, in Montreal, clubs like the Lime Light continued to thrive as dens of bad music, bad fashion, and lots and lots of cocaine.

The 1980s Expos contained some of the best partiers in baseball. While Mickey Mantle and Whitey Ford, and Babe Ruth and Paul Waner before them, had burnt the candle at both ends, they had done so on all-American beer and liquor. These were new times, with new vices. Coke was now the drug of choice – at least, the choice of some of the Expos.

Cocaine was popular in the United States as well, but the new drug was especially plentiful in Montreal. The Montreal mob, an inclusive consortium of Italian, Irish, and biker gangs, were old hands at drug trafficking. Heroin had been their main commodity in the 1950s and 1960s, but customer demand had changed their focus. As Montreal was a port city, and the mob controlled the docks, it was not difficult to move the product in through shipping.

Later, everyone in Montreal, even amateurs, would get in on the boom times. In 1981, a bunch of Montreal schoolteachers got busted traveling back from Peru with two and a half kilos of coke. By 1985, this was pennyante stuff: the Montreal police found 23 kilos, worth $20 million Canadian, in the trunk of a car. In the early '90s, a private plane was seized on a local Quebec airfield carrying 3 metric tons of the stuff, with a street value of $1 billion.

Yes, it was the golden era of cocaine, and Montreal was Canada's version of Miami. Montreal was such a coke town that *players from other teams* would resupply there. Whitey Herzog, the manager of St. Louis at the time, confessed that the situation was so bad in Montreal that he changed the travel schedule for the Cards' trips to play there. Rather than the usual practice of arriving in the city the night before the first game of the series, Whitey had the Cardinals arrive the same day as the first game. That way, he figured, he'd get at least one clear-eyed game out of his team before they hit the Montreal disco scene that night to refill their prescriptions.

It was little wonder then that some of the Expos would take a dive, nose-first, right into the party. One of them was Tim Raines. Tim had cups of coffee with the Expos in '79 and '80, but in his first full season in 1981, he tore it up, hitting .304 and swiping a league-leading 71 bags. He would finish second in Rookie of the Year voting.

In that first year, freed from the drudgery and penury of playing minor league baseball, Tim was like a kid in a candy store. The problem was, the candy was nose candy. He became addicted to the point that he would carry cocaine in his uniform to use during games. He later admitted that he developed his trademark headfirst slide, not from style or strategy, but because he didn't want to risk breaking the glass vial of coke he was carrying in his back pocket. The stuff was expensive.

In 1982, his batting average fell to .277. He later admitted that he had spent at least $40,000 – about half his salary – that year on cocaine. Raines would eventually, with the help and friendship of Andre Dawson playing a major role, get his act together and go on to enjoy a Hall of Fame career.

The next partaker would be Ellis Valentine. In the Cooperstown wing for Wasted Talent, Ellis Valentine would be a first ballot selection. The Expos brought him up at age 21 for good, and he rewarded their optimism with a .279 line in 305 at-bats. Preternaturally gifted with raw athletic ability, he was one of the top fielding right fielders in baseball, with a cannon for an arm. It was death to try to go first to third on him, and eventually they stopped trying. His manager, Felipe Alou, summed up his arm: "There's a plateau where you can't throw the ball any harder and you can't be any more accurate. That was Ellis Valentine."

In 1977, he hit .293 and slugged .504, followed with a nearly identical year in '78. But by 1979, Ellis was in full-blown party mode. On a road trip to Los Angeles, shortly before batting practice, a sports car pulled up outside the entrance to the visitor's clubhouse. The car's passenger door opened, and someone pushed a comatose Valentine out onto the pavement. The car sped away, and someone dragged the body into the clubhouse.

The effects didn't seem to show up in his game. In 1980, Valentine was on pace for his typical year, hitting .297 and slugging .487. Then, on May 30, he took a fastball to the face from the Cardinals' Roy Thomas.

To this day, Ellis maintains that the beaning was intentional, ordered by none other than the aforementioned Whitey Herzog. Allegedly, Herzog believed – incorrectly, according to Ellis – that Ellis was personally supplying the Cardinals with cocaine, and so he ordered Thomas to deliver a message. The message broke Valentine's cheekbone in six places.

Did Valentine's lack of sobriety contribute to the inability to dodge the pitch? He would never confirm or deny it, but it's hard not to wonder if he weren't as clear-eyed as he could have been. But nonetheless, he missed a critical six weeks.

In 1981, the partying finally caught up to him. He started the season ice-cold at the plate. Only a 3-for-3 day on the last day of April pulled his average above the Mendoza line. By late May, he was traded to the Mets. He was even worse for them. While he bounced back a little in 1982, his career was effectively over. He missed all of 1984 with what was supposedly a bruised heel. The Rangers gave him a last chance in 1985, but after 11 games, they too had seen enough. He was out of baseball at age 30. Like Raines, Valentine would eventually beat his addiction, and now works as an addiction counselor.

Then there's Ron LeFlore. LeFlore's lone season with the Expos was 1980, but he really, really enjoyed himself. A former .300 hitter with Detroit, his drug-addled year with Montreal resulted in a .257 line.

LeFlore's best story involved his chase for the league lead in stolen bases. Cocaine hadn't affected his ability to steal bases. On the last day of the season, LeFlore had 95 stolen bags, but he wasn't in the lineup. But the Phillies' Pete Rose informed him, during the game, that he only needed two steals to win the stolen base championship that year. That got Ron's attention. He wanted to get in the game and get that record.

The only problem was that Rose told LeFlore this in the Phillies' clubhouse, where Ron was partying. He put down his champagne and emerged, blinking from the sunlight – from the opponent's dugout – and went in the game as a pinch runner. He stole second, then third to secure the stolen base crown, and promptly went back to partying with the Phillies.

So really who cares about the partying 'Spos? Just some guys having too much of a good time, right? Well, maybe karma cares. Because what the partiers didn't know, or didn't want to know, was that the party was being paid for in blood.

That coke was coming from Colombia, and the guy who was supplying all that coke was the most murderous bastard on the planet, one Pablo Emilio Escobar Gaviria. It is estimated that at one time 80 percent of the cocaine being smuggled into the United States was being supplied by Escobar and his Medellin cartel.

He made Forbes Magazine's list of the world's top ten billionaires. Despite his attempt to portray himself as a Robin Hood figure with well-publicized charitable donations, the fact remains that his vast empire was built on thousands and thousands of dead bodies. And it was all fueled by the endless hunger of cocaine users in North America.

Escobar first began killing his rival druglords and their crews. Then he began killing Colombian policemen and soldiers. Then, Colombian politicians and judges. His hitman, John Jairo Velasquez Vasquez, who went by the *nom de guerre* of "Popeye," admitted to committing 300 murders by himself, and ordering at least 3,000 others.

They killed the Colombia Minister of Justice, a Supreme Court Justice, and the Attorney General. Then, for good measure, the cartel killed the Minister of Justice who had replaced the one that they just killed.

In 1989, a Colombian politician named Luis Carlos Galán was nominated by the nation's Liberal Party as its presidential candidate. Galán saw no hope for Colombia as long as Escobar was its *de facto* king. With remarkable courage, Galán openly and repeatedly called for the extradition of Escobar to the United States to stand trial. When it looked like Galán might win, Escobar simply ordered his death. Galán was shot by Escobar's thugs at a political rally, as he took the stage to give a speech in front of thousands of supporters.

Galán's chief advisor, Cesar Gaviria, was nominated to take his place. Undaunted by his boss's assassination, Gaviria also promised to support Escobar's extradition. Escobar ordered a bomb to be placed on a plane Gaviria was scheduled to be on. Gaviria was lucky: his security detail had been warned of possible danger and pulled him off the plane minutes before takeoff. The bomb exploded in mid-air and killed all 110 passengers. That's how cold-blooded Escobar was – 110 innocent human lives were of no consequence, as long as he could kill one person that he wanted to get at the same time.

At one point, the Medellin cartel was killing so many people *that the hospitals ran out of room to store the bodies.*

Escobar's body count was in the thousands, but his indirect influence resulted in tens of thousands of additional deaths. His cocaine, and disputes over the right to distribute it, prompted turf wars between rival gangs in every country where his product was being sold. Enormous profits were at stake. The same massacres taking place in Colombia were playing out in America and the rest of the world, all tracing back to Pablo Escobar's white powder. In Miami alone, the "Cocaine Cowboy Wars" resulted in hundreds, maybe thousands, of murders, all of which can also be laid at Escobar's door.

So the Expos – some of them anyway – were basically buying this monster's product, and his profits were literally funding the deaths of tens of thousands of people worldwide.

Is that enough for a curse? It should be.

Except the same could be said for dozens, if not hundreds, of players on other baseball teams. The Expos could hardly bear the blame alone for the behavior that many of the other teams were also witnessing.

Indeed, the Pittsburgh Pirates had their own very special moment in the spotlight in 1985, when a half dozen current and former Pirates were called before a federal grand jury to testify about their drug use. The Pirates weren't the only guests of honor. There were Cardinals and Yankees and Mets and Tigers and Giants and Braves and Padres whose prolific drug habits were dragged out of the clubhouse and into semi-public view. The Expos didn't miss out, as Tim Raines was called before the grand jury as well. Heck, even the guy in the Pirates' parrot mascot was involved – he was the main supplier to the Pittsburgh players. When the FBI came knocking at his door, the Parrot did what parrots do – he squawked. To avoid prosecution, he agreed to wear a wire to record drug transactions. It isn't clear whether he was wearing the Parrot costume during the undercover work.

So we can't really blame the Nationals Curse on the partying Expos. But there's another reason that the Nationals Curse can't be traced to Pablo Escobar. That's because the Escobar curse belongs to the Colombian national soccer team.

Escobar's greatest passion, other than killing people, was soccer. He bought Colombia's top professional team, Atlética Nacional, and pumped millions of dollars into making them a premier South American side. (An intended side benefit of the purchase was that it allowed millions of dollars of cocaine profits to be laundered through the business of the team.)

Sometime, he could combine his two hobbies of soccer and murder. For example, when Atlética Nacional lost a match due to some questionable officiating, there was speculation that a rival drug lord had bribed the referee. Escobar simply had the referee assassinated.

He paid the top Colombian soccer players, and even international stars like Diego Maradona, to come play in pickup games with him and his lieutenants, or just to party. Even more than he loved Atlética, he loved the Colombian national team, known as *Los Cafeteros*, the "Coffee Growers," after Colombia's second most successful product.

In the early '90s, the Colombian government finally had had enough and went after Escobar full-bore. Escobar saw the writing on the wall. What he didn't want was to be extradited to the United States, where the death penalty or life without parole awaited him. So he made the Colombian government a deal. He would surrender and agree to be imprisoned in Colombia. There was one small caveat: he would agree to be imprisoned in a luxury "prison" that he would not only build, but also run. It was a palace, free of any guards, where he and dozens of his henchmen dined on the best food and wine, visited regularly by trucked-in hookers. Rather than take him into custody in a violent arrest, the Colombian government agreed to the bizarre arrangement.

The prison, called *La Catedral*, included, of course, a soccer field. When Escobar invited the Colombia national soccer team to come up and play soccer with him, they happily obliged.

The public was outraged. Here was the national team, the pride and joy of every Colombian, perhaps the most important national symbol for its people, being tipped in drug money to play a pickup game with Escobar, the man who had butchered thousands of Colombians, and who supposedly was serving a prison term. Perhaps they couldn't pass up the money. Maybe they were too scared to refuse. But the Colombia national team has been saddled with a curse since its association with Pablo, a curse that can rightfully take its place with any in sports.

In 1993, the Colombian government decided to put an end to Pablo's cushy life at *La Catedral*. They sent in the military to seize him and put him and his henchmen in a real prison, perhaps even to extradite them to the USA. When they arrived, Pablo was gone. Warned of the approach of the army, he had slipped out. He was on the lam.

Escobar was finally gunned down by the Colombian military in December 1993 in a Medellin slum. He was wearing soccer cleats. He would not get to see *Los Cafeteros* play in the 1994 World Cup six months later. But his curse would make its presence known.

For the 1994 World Cup, Colombia's team was perhaps the greatest side the country had ever assembled. *Los Cafeteros* had rampaged through their qualifying group like a juggernaut. After five qualifying matches, Colombia had yet to lose a game. In the group final, they had to play their archrival, Argentina, the 800-pound gorilla of South American soccer. Argentina had won the World Cup in 1978, then won it again in 1986. In 1990, they had merely come in second.

Even worse, Colombia would face Argentina in the critical final game in Buenos Aires, before 40,000 screaming Argentine fans. But Colombia dropped a thrashing on the favored Argentinians. It was an unprecedented blowout: 5-0. It would be the equivalent of winning a playoff baseball game 15-0. Now expectations for the team were sky-high; many picked *Los Cafeteros* to win the Cup.

Cue Tantalus. Disaster struck. In their opening World Cup game, perhaps overconfident, they lost, 2-0, to an unheralded Romanian team. That made their next game a must-win. Fortunately, it was against the United States, not a significant threat to the superior Colombian side.

In the game against the USA, late in the second half, Colombia's star defender Andres Escobar (no relation to Pablo) attempted to clear a ball near his own goal. He spun and drove the ball, not out of bounds, but directly into his own goal. The own goal proved to be the difference, as both teams scored one more goal apiece, and the USA won, 2-1.

Andres Escobar was a national hero, perhaps the best player on the Colombian team, as well as the most popular. Escobar's own goal was as rare as it was tragic. Only nine times before, in sixty-four years of World Cup matches, had an own goal decided a match.

Colombia was eliminated, and Andres Escobar returned to his home in Medellin, Colombia. Five days after the own goal, he was leaving a nightclub when three gunman approached him in a parking lot and shot him dead. Pablo Escobar was dead, but other Colombian drug kingpins had wagered heavily on Colombia and lost. The nation mourned the murdered player, but Pablo's shadow had fallen on him and his unlucky play.

Thereafter, Colombia's national team would assemble the following record of woe:

1998 World Cup: defeated in first round
2002 World Cup: did not qualify
2006 World Cup: did not qualify
2010 World Cup: did not qualify
2014 World Cup: lost in quarter-finals to Brazil

In the 2018 World Cup, in the round of 16, Colombia tied England 1-1 in regulation. It went to penalty kicks. England is known as a team that doesn't win shootouts. In its soccer history, England had lost six of seven shootouts, including five in a row.

After four attempts each, the teams were tied with three goals apiece. On the fifth attempt, the English keeper made a diving stop, and the English player netted his shot. Colombia loses, on penalty kicks, 4-3. Tantalus strikes again.

Yes, the ghost of Pablo Escobar haunts the Colombians, not the Nationals. Different sport, different country. We will have to keep looking.

CHAPTER 9

The Curse of the Mascot

BUT THE DRUG-DEALING PIRATES PARROT gives me another thought that bears exploring. Could a mascot be the source of the Curse of the Nationals?

We've established that the Expo/Nats didn't really have a phenomenal player that was traded away to start a curse. There's no report of anyone on the Expos taking bribes, like the White Sox, to throw games. And, as far as I know, no record of exulting Expos fans dumping a statue of Ronald McDonald in the St. Lawrence. But what about a mascot issue? After all, the start of the Cubs' Billy Goat curse was due to a mascot. Granted, Murphy the goat was the mascot of the Billy Goat Tavern, not of the Cubs proper, but he was a mascot nonetheless. So we need to ponder: could an errant mascot be the cause of the Curse of the Nationals?

Certainly, the Nationals' current mascot is one appropriate to a team doomed to failure. You see, I was, unfortunately, present for the birth of "Screech."

The Nationals' inaugural season was upon us, and all seemed right with the world. For the first time in three and a half decades, there would be baseball in Washington, DC. Real baseball too, not that coach-pitch American League stuff.

I was giddy. I had been a baseball fan since the late 1960s, but had never lived in a town with a professional baseball team. My spectating as a kid had been confined to a once-a-year pilgrimage from South Carolina to Atlanta, the closest baseball city to us, to see the Braves play. Now the aweing potential of eighty-one games a year awaited me, a Metro ride away. This was a dream come true, truly.

Moreover, my children were going to have a better life than I had, in terms of baseball. Thus, in April of 2005, the inaugural Washington season, I took my kids to RFK Stadium to watch the national pastime.

We got to our seats early, as I usually try to do. It was Kids' Day or something, and they had invited a half dozen mascots, from various other teams, who were committing assorted acts of tomfoolery in the outfield. And I noticed an egg sitting in centerfield. A six foot high, giant, plush egg.

Suddenly, over the loudspeakers, the announcer boomed: "And we are proud to welcome all these mascots, who have come here to witness the birth of the Washington Nationals' new mascot!"

Yeah, okay, whatever. The attendant mascots dance around the egg, appearing to be mesmerized by the egg and what it could possibly contain. I can only think of the dwarves dancing around the tiny Stonehenge in Spinal Tap.

The announcer is unfazed by the crowd's utter lack of interest in the goings-on in the outfield: "Yes, here is Doofus from the University of So-and-So! And Generic Dog from Local College! And Badly Sewn Mascot from our minor league team at Harrisburg!" Each one takes a bow. Not a soul is paying attention. People continue to buy hotdogs and find their seats.

Now the announcer wants us to know, here comes the big reveal. "WAIT! WHAT IS HAPPENING?" The furries gather around the egg, craning their heads, feigning a burning intrigue, unshared by anyone in the stands.

"THERE SEEMS TO BE SOME MOVEMENT IN THE EGG! WAIT! DO I SEE A CRACK!"

The furries mime surprise and fascination. Somewhere, in the afterlife, Marcel Marceau is regretting his life's work.

The giant plush egg begins to quiver and rise. The top half of the egg falls away and out walks a man in a scrawny bald eagle suit.

Now the announcer, like we're at professional wrestling: "LADIES AND GENTLEMEN, PLEASE WELCOME ….. "

"SCREEEEEEECH!"

My kids, then aged nine to fourteen, are bored out of their minds. And all I can think is: "You knew over five months ago that the team was coming here. You had five months to come up with something ---- and this is it?"

Wow, a bald eagle. How original. Because he is basically a near carbon copy of "Slapshot," who is 1) also a bald eagle mascot of 2) another Washington team, the NHL's Washington Capitals. Oh, wait. There is also "Talon," who is 1) also a bald eagle mascot of 2) another Washington team, MLS's D.C. United. So, if you were trying to come up with the most clichéd mascot possible for a Washington-based team, mission accomplished.

The lamest mascot in the bigs, Screech. *Photo by author.*

The Nationals reveal later, seemingly with pride, that Screech was the suggestion of one of its fans, an eight-year-old fan who scribbled something on a piece of paper that became Screech. There's a reason kids aren't allowed to vote or drive or do anything of consequence. If there's a lamer major league mascot than Screech, I haven't seen it.

Yes, Screech is so original that not one but two minor league hockey teams have the same mascot. The Cape Breton Screaming Eagles, of the Quebec Montreal Junior Hockey League, also have an Eagle named Screech as their mascot. The belated Springfield Falcons of the American Hockey League, before their move in 2016 to Tucson to become the Roadrunners, featured their own version of Screech, only with blue "feathers" instead of white. Again, this is what happens when you turn over your marketing to an eight-year-old: you wind up with the same trite mascot as two minor league hockey teams, who probably only spent a couple of thousand dollars to come up with the same stupid bird.

The tragedy is that the Nationals missed a chance to bring with them a truly epic mascot, a mascot for the ages. Yes, I speak of Youppi!

Yes, the Montreal Expos had a mascot, a real one, and not some hackneyed bird. Youppi!! (the first exclamation point is not mine --- it's actually part of his name. The second one is mine.)

In the 1970s, the Padres introduced the San Diego Chicken mascot, and the Phillies introduced the Philly Phanatic. Despite the objections of baseball purists, these mascots' antics seemed to be well received by the home crowds. As success breeds imitation, soon every baseball team believed it needed a dehydrated man in a plushie Muppet costume to render similar hijinks in its stands.

The Expos were no exception. In 1978, they first had trotted out Souki, a mascot who looked like Mr. Met's cousin, if his cousin were an anorexic astronaut. Souki was met with such dismay (kids were apparently terrified of him) that he was deep-sixed after one season. Then the Expos wised up and hired the same lady who had stitched up the Philly Phanatic. And Youppi! (which doesn't mean "yuppie," but is how "Yippee!" is spelled *en Francais*) was born.

Youppi! was immediately a hit, as much a success as Souki had been a disaster. Youppi! had a vaguely humanoid face, but the rest of him was covered in bright orange fur. Imagine if the Brewers' Bernie Brewer and the Flyers' Gritty had a love child. An Expos jersey and cap completed his outfit.

But the real source of Youppi!'s fame is that he holds a baseball record that will likely never be broken. He is the only mascot to ever be thrown out of a major league baseball game.

It was August 23, 1989, and the Dodgers were in town. Pascual Perez, for the Expos, and Orel Hershiser, for the Dodgers, were both dealing that night. After nine innings, no one had scored --- extra innings.

Youppi! did his usual routine for a late night, extra inning game. He went and put on *les pyjamas* and returned to continue his antics. The tenth inning came and went: no one scored. Then, in the 11th, Youppi! decided to dance on the Dodgers' dugout, ending in a belly flop.

Tommy Lasorda, the Dodgers' manager, was having none of it. There is a legend that Tommy was asleep in the dugout (in truth, a not uncommon event), and he was grumpy because Youppi!'s antics had disturbed his slumber. In any event, Lasorda groggily emerged from the dugout. He complained to the home plate umpire, demanding that Youppi! be ejected. And the umpire obliged. Youppi!, as they say in baseball, was run.

However, Youppi!'s banishment was rescinded a couple of innings later, upon the condition that he behave himself. He returned to the stadium, but didn't grace the roof of the Dodgers' dugout again. Youppi! probably wished he had stayed tossed. The Expos lost, 1-0, in 22 innings on a Rick Dempsey homer.[21] But the legend of Youppi!, the outlaw mascot, the only mascot ever to get the old heave-ho in a major league game, was forever established.

---

21. Current Nats skipper Davey Martinez played center field for the Expos for every inning of that marathon. He went 1 for 6, with two strikeouts and two walks, plus an error.

When the Expos became the Nats, the team still retained the rights to Youppi!. But rather than bring in the most spirited mascot in the history of the game, we got --- Screech. It's like the difference between watching Elvis and watching some old guy butcher "All Shook Up" at karaoke night.

A mascot of Youppi!'s caliber was not going to be unemployed. When the Nationals gave him his walking papers, he was immediately snatched up by the Montreal Canadiens. Donning a Canadiens sweater rather than an Expos jersey since 2005, he is, as far as I know, the only mascot ever to jump from one team to another, and the only mascot to jump from one sport to another.

Could it be Youppi!? Can the Curse be due to Youppi!? If the Nationals ditch their current abomination of a mascot and take back Youppi!, is all forgiven, and the Curse abated?

Well, in examining previous suspects, we've established that since Blue Monday is evidence of the existence of the Curse, that means, obviously, that the cause of the Curse has to predate Blue Monday, October 19, 1981. And Youppi! was certainly there for Blue Monday --- he began his career as Montreal's mascot in the 1979 season. He would have been a seasoned veteran by Blue Monday in October 1981.

So Youppi! has the longevity to be in play as the cause of the Curse. But what is the sin against Youppi!, or what offense did Youppi! commit? What travesty has Youppi! committed, or what travesty has been committed upon Youppi!?

There doesn't seem to be any. The only thing that I can come up with is what we've just discussed, the Nationals shabbily discarding a mascot of legend, the vaunted Youppi!, in favor of the half-baked, deplorable Screech. That debacle happened in 2005, far, far too late to play a part in the Curse of the Nationals.

And, truth be told, Youppi! has not been exactly tearing it up for the Canadiens. After winning the Stanley Cup in four straight years, 1976-1979, then again in 1986 and 1993, the Habs have yet to even reach the finals since. This isn't due to Youppi! --- in the eleven seasons between their last Stanley Cup and Youppi!'s arrival, they didn't even make the playoffs for five of them. Still, Youppi! has brought them very little in the way of improvement. They've logged thirteen full seasons with Youppi! on board, and they have still missed the playoff in five of those.

Youppi!, we hardly knew ye. The search for a scapegoat continues.

CHAPTER 10

The Curse of the Quebecois

So we discussed Rusty Staub, and we've discussed cocaine. We've even tried to pin it on a mascot. What about the Expos' banishment from Canada? How did that come about?

Why did the Washington Nationals even come to exist? Because the Montreal Expos died.

Why did the Expos die?

Because of Bill 101.

You see, as it turns out, Montreal is in Quebec. And Quebec, it seems, has a split personality. That split personality caused the demise of the Expos.

Montreal was founded by French missionaries and traders in the 17th century, and flourished as a French colony for a century and a half. But in 1763, after the Seven Years' War, France and England signed the Treaty of Paris, by which France yielded all claims to Canada to the English. This was all well and good – except for the French colonists and their descendants. Those French citizens, although abandoned by their nation, still composed a majority of the new province of Lower Canada (roughly what is now Quebec), but were politically and economically disadvantaged under English rule. As a result, they, and their descendants, have been trying to undo that Treaty ever since.

For example, in 1837, Canadians of French descent organized the *Parti Patriote* to protest their treatment at the hands of the British. When their political petitions were rejected, they formed a paramilitary force, and open rebellion ensued. The Patriotes defeated a small British force at Saint-Denis, only to be defeated by the British reinforcements. The Patriotes even inspired the formation of like-minded "Hunters' Lodges" in northern towns in the United States, secret organizations willing to support the Patriotes with arms and soldiers. The Lodges, which were composed of a handful of French-Canadian exiles and a fair number of Americans, either sympathetic to their cause or just hankering for a good adventure, launched futile freebooting "invasions" of Canada from Vermont, New York, and Michigan.

Taking a page from their more successful neighbors to the south, the Patriotes declared independence from Britain. On February 22, 1838, a Patriote rebel, Robert Nelson, hiding in Vermont from the Canadian authorities, penned the "Declaration of Independence of Lower Canada," written *en Francais* of course. The Hunters then proceeded to elect a Canadian government in exile, in Cleveland. It seemed to include mostly Americans as its Founding Fathers. Nathan Williams, a wholesale grocer from Cleveland, had the honor of being the first, and only, Vice-President of the French Republic of Canada.

When the rebellion was finally quelled in late 1838, the British response was punitive and ugly. Most of the captured rebels were sentenced to life imprisonment in the British Empire's jail-country, Australia, but several were shot without trial. Other of the rebel leaders were tried, sentenced to death, and hanged. British troops and loyalist militia wreaked vengeance on villages that were viewed as sympathetic to the rebels; unknown numbers of non-combatants were killed or savaged in vendettas by anti-rebel mobs.

The French-Canadians still remember. Successful or not, to this day the rebellion of 1838 is celebrated in Quebec with its own provincial holiday. While the rest of Canada is celebrating "Victoria Day," Quebec celebrates the third Monday of May as "National Patriots Day."

The British solution to this unpleasantness was to merge the two provinces of Lower Canada (Quebec, more or less) and Upper Canada (Ontario, more or less) into a single province under the Act of Union, passed in 1840. This did not, as we will see, assuage the Frenchies. The Act gave equal number of parliamentary seats to the Lower Canadians as the Upper Canadians. As there were roughly 650,000 citizens of Lower Canada (i.e., French) and only 450,000 citizens of Upper Canada (i.e., Brits), the "equal representation" meant, in practice, that a French vote was worth just two-thirds of that of an English vote. More critically, the Act's unspoken goal was clear for all to see: to slowly exorcise the French culture from the Canadian body entirely. The Act of Union was intended to Anglicize almost all aspects of Canadian life. The French language was banned from official government use, including in the provincial legislature. Even French-language schools were subject to new restrictions. The English intended to complete, through cultural assimilation, the conquest of the French that had taken place almost a century earlier. Willy-nilly, their French descendants would be brought to heel, and become proper Englishmen.[22]

After the Act of Union, the Quebecois continued to chafe under their status as second-class citizens in the British regime. They viewed the goal of the British, not inaccurately, as the eradication in Canada not only of French language, history, and culture, but of their Catholic religion. For decades, while there were no outright rebellions, the Francophones' cause continued to simmer in Quebec. Some French-Canadians openly called for parts of Canada to leave the British Empire and be annexed to the United States.

Isolated outbursts of French-English violence did arise, such as those during World War I. Even though the battles of the First World War raged in the fields of France, Quebec's historically-French citizenry felt unmoved by the government's calls for Canadians to patriotically "serve the British Empire." Most were reluctant to volunteer, and many failed

---

22. Today in Montreal, its residents are divided, in local parlance, into "French" and "English." "French" means those of French descent – primarily, it signifies those who speak French at home. "English" means everyone else of European descent, including Italian, Portuguese, Polish, and Russian. This can prove baffling to members of those ethnic groups who don't have a single English drop of blood and don't enjoy the misclassification.

to report when drafted. In 1918, French resentment over conscription efforts in Quebec reached a flashpoint. Recruiting officers were chased by mobs out of Francophone neighborhoods. When national police tried to arrest a suspected draft dodger in Quebec City, riots broke out. Martial law was declared, and thousands of English-speaking troops were rushed from other provinces to quell the revolt.

On Easter weekend, the rioting continued unabated, with tens of thousands of participants destroying police stations and recruitment offices. The uprising ultimately led to the British troops firing on a crowd. Five rioters were killed and over 150 injured.

While few similar eruptions of violence took place in the years after the conscription riots of 1918, the idea of Quebec gaining independence from Canada – the separatist movement – continued to thrive in the minds of many French-Canadians. Finally, in the 1960s, things in Montreal took a turn for the decidedly violent. A separatist group emerged, known as *Front de Libération du Québec*, or FLQ, that decided it was not enough to hold political debates on the idea of Quebec nationalism. It was time to force the Canadian government to negotiate the independence of Quebec.

They were quite willing to engage in terrorism to reach their ends. FLQ launched a campaign of bombing in Montreal. At first, the bombs were deployed for the destruction of property only. But in 1968, its tactics changed. The number of bombings skyrocketed, with 52 bombs in that year alone. Then, on February 13, 1969, they set off a large bomb at the Montreal Stock Exchange, which seriously injured 27 people.

Finally, in 1970, they kidnapped James Richard Cross, the British Trade Commissioner, and then kidnapped the Vice-Premier of Quebec, Pierre Laporte. While Cross was eventually released after two months of captivity, Laporte was murdered. His dead body was found in the trunk of one of the kidnapper's cars.

The escalation of violence, especially Laporte's murder, was the downfall of FLQ. The Canadian government responded with an intensive anti-terrorism crackdown, which captured numerous FLQ bigwigs and drove the rest underground. More critically, FLQ's campaign of mayhem cost it any popular support its cause had enjoyed.

Meanwhile, the Parti Quebecois (PQ) had formed in 1968 as a merger of two separatist political parties, and now championed itself as a civil, political alternative to the violence of groups like FLQ. In the provincial elections of 1970, PQ won just seven seats out of 110. But the French-Canadian voters soon responded to PQ's message, and quickly adopted the party as the champion of their long-aggrieved status. Just six years later, in 1976, Parti Quebecois captured almost two-thirds of the 110 parliamentary seats, and by itself formed the official government of the province of Quebec.

As the party in control, the Parti Quebecois's first act was to introduce, and pass, Bill 101, known as "the Charter of the French Language." Bill 101 established that the official language of Quebec was French. Henceforth, all official proceedings – legislative, executive, or judicial – had to be conducted in French.

More critically to the numerous businesses employing persons in Quebec, Bill 101 required that businesses conduct their internal communications in French. It was now a violation of the law to require employees to know English. The law even established a language police, *Office québécois de la langue française,* which was empowered to investigate failures to conduct business in French, and was authorized to punish, with exorbitant fines, those caught using English instead of French.

The effect on the economy of the province was immediate. Businesses, already skittish from the FLQ violence, fled in droves. Within months of Bill 101 becoming law, most companies that had their headquarters in Montreal moved them out of the province. One of the first to go was The Royal Bank of Canada, the largest corporation in the country. Then Sun Life, one of the largest insurance conglomerates in the world, and the proud owner of Montreal's biggest skyscraper, announced it would be moving its corporate headquarters from Montreal to Toronto, taking some 2000 jobs with it. That announcement alone created a massive sell-off in the Montreal Stock Exchange, dubbed – what else? – Black Friday.

Company after company followed suit. The final insult? The Bank of Montreal, Canada's oldest bank, moved its corporate headquarters to Toronto. That's right. The Bank of Montreal left Montreal.

Bill 101 was the final revenge of the French-Canadians, and the final straw in the death of baseball in Montreal. It killed Montreal's long-held position as the financial and industrial center of Canada. After the bill's passing in 1977, Toronto would be the unquestioned center of Canadian business.

Fleeing with all the jobs were the Expos' hopes of survival. Fans are people, and people need jobs. Those jobs migrated, tens of thousands of them, when Bill 101 passed. The fans followed. Sports franchises also need a healthy business climate in their city in order to prosper. Corporations buy tickets, corporations buy advertisements, and corporations pay money to make partnerships with franchises. Due to Bill 101, those corporations picked up, packed their bags, and headed to Toronto, where the Blue Jays opened their arms wide.

And so Bill 101 killed the Expos. And the Quebec separatist movement caused Bill 101. And the Treaty of Paris in 1763, whereby France ceded Canada to Great Britain at the end of the French and Indian War, caused the Quebec separatist movement.

But what caused the Treaty of Paris? At last, we may be getting warm.

CHAPTER 11

The War Of The Conquest

WHEN THE TREATY OF PARIS was signed in 1763, ending the Seven Years' War, all French claims to Canada or to any lands east of the Mississippi River were ceded to Britain. But nonetheless, Frenchmen remained in Canada, mostly in Quebec, and refused to kowtow to their British overlords. Two hundred and fifty years of simmering friction later, their descendants had their revenge on the conquerors, and killed Montreal's baseball team in the process. So what caused this running sore of French-Canadian resentment and turmoil?

A long, long time ago, France and England had a tiff – a misunderstanding that lasted about five centuries. Between the 13th and 18th centuries, they had almost a dozen separate full-blown wars. They even had a War that lasted over a Hundred Years.

For the first few centuries, these military conflicts were geographically limited to the European continent. Then came the Age of Exploration. When Christopher Columbus came back with tales of a New World, ripe for the plucking, every European nation took notice and immediately sought to join the plunder awaiting across the Atlantic.

A mere five years after Columbus's discovery, an English ship piloted by an Italian captain named Giovanni Caboto landed in Newfoundland, or Prince Edward Island (the actual landing site is in dispute, as several provinces vie for the honor). Caboto, better known by his Anglicized name of John Cabot, was seeking the legendary Northwest Passage, a short cut from Europe through North America to the rich trading possibilities with China and the Spice Islands. Under the rules of colonization then in play, Cabot claimed the entire land, by right of discovery, as the possession of King Henry VII of England, the sponsor of his voyage.

Despite Cabot's discovery, the English did little to exploit their claim to Canada. To be sure, not all nations viewed the English claim as dispositive. Nearly forty years later, the French king sent an expedition to Canada under Jacques Cartier. Cartier also sought to discover the Northwest Passage. While Cabot's landing had been little more than a toe-touch on the Canadian mainland, Cartier was determined to go further inland in search of the route to the Far East.

He sailed his ship, the *Grande Hermine,* into the Gulf of St. Lawrence and landed at Gaspé Bay on July 24, 1534, where he planted a 30-foot-tall cross to claim the land for the King of France. Buoyed by his success, Cartier was given another expedition to lead the following year. This time, he decided to go much further inland, and sailed up the St. Lawrence River for several hundred miles. There, on a prominent hill, he found an Iroquois settlement called Hochelaga.

Cartier would make a third voyage to Canada, but thereafter French interest in the New World waned. It would not be until seventy years later, in 1611, that another French explorer, Samuel Champlain, returned to Hochelaga and started a trading post on an island next to the village. Another thirty years later, a group of Frenchmen set sail to establish a permanent colony in the area. On May 17, 1642, they landed on the southern shore of the island and founded a settlement. As good Catholics, they named it after the Mother of God – Ville-Marie.

The French settlement was quickly besieged by steady and ferocious Indian attacks. Ten years after its founding, the population of Ville-Marie had been reduced to the point where its abandonment was seriously contemplated. But by the late 17th century, bolstered by additional waves of colonists, and a booming fur trade with the local Indian tribes, Ville-Marie was here to stay.

Eventually the name of the settlement was changed. The original Iroquois village of Hochelaga had been near a tall hill about two miles from the St. Lawrence River. Jacques Cartier had named the hill "the Royal Mount" in honor of his sponsor, the King of France: in French, "Mont Royal," which was transmogrified, thanks to a Spanish-speaking mapmaker, into "Montreal."

Cabot's claim for the King of England had preceded the French claim by forty years. But under the well-known legal doctrine of "You snooze, you lose," the French had ignored the English claim and laid their own on top of it. They called their colony "New France." While assorted English attempts to start colonies in Newfoundland and Nova Scotia all ended in failure, the French settlements at Montreal and Quebec City thrived. Yet the unresolved and competing claims of England and France would ferment over the next hundred years. That simmering issue would lead, perhaps, to the Curse of the Nationals.

The conflicts between the kingdoms of England and France had not abated since the Hundred Years' War and Joan of Arc. Again, the English and French military actions in these wars were still largely confined to the European continent, with sporadic naval battles where the combatants happened to encounter each other on the seas. As the countries expanded their footprints to include colonies discovered or conquered, the two enemies expanded the theater of conflict to include their colonial settlements and trading posts throughout the world. This led to military actions in India, the West Indies, South America --- and Canada.

For example, in Queen Anne's War (1702-1713), the North American colonists of the two dueling nations decided that they wanted to join the fun that was going on in Europe. English settlers from New England captured settlements in Nova Scotia, and even launched an abortive invasion of Quebec. The Indian allies of the French invaded Massachusetts and burned the town of Deerfield to the ground; they killed 56 English settlers and took over a hundred back as captives.

After Queen Anne's War ended in 1713, the rivals sought to use the peace to strengthen their holds on the continent. The French built forts on Lake Champlain, on Cape Breton Island, at Niagara Falls and in the

Ohio Valley. The British extended their thrusts deeper into Nova Scotia and Maine, and English traders pushed west over the Appalachian mountains from Virginia and Pennsylvania.

Next came the War of the Austrian Succession (1740-48), and the renewed French-English conflict again spilled over from Europe into armed struggles between Britain's American colonies and French forces in Canada. Both sides sent raiding parties across the border. A collection of freebooters from Boston sailed to Cape Breton Island and took its main fort, Louisbourg, after a siege of several weeks. France launched a gigantic hundred-ship fleet to retake Louisburg, intending to sack Boston in retaliation along the way, but luckily for that city, the fleet never reached North America. In 1748, the belligerents, exhausted by almost a decade of hostilities, signed the Treaty of Aix-la-Chappelle, which ended the war. It did not, however, resolve the conflict between the two countries' ambitions in North America.

The French and British competing claims for territory in the New World were not confined to Canada. Of potentially greater concern was the valuable Ohio Valley. France's claims to the Valley stemmed from LaSalle's exploration of the Mississippi River in the 1680s. Under the rules of conquest-by-exploration that the civilized nations of Europe recognized, LaSalle, as the first European to visit the Mississippi River, established France's claim to not only the River, but all tributary rivers and streams that fed into it, and all lands that were adjacent to or drained by those tributaries. This territory therefore included all land between the crest of the Appalachian mountain range in the East and the Rocky Mountain range in the West. LaSalle had named this huge French claim "Louisiana," after his patron, the King of France.

The British maintained that their claim, established through their American colonies, traveled west as far as the landmass continued. Thus, their colony of Virginia, to their mind, was not its present circumscribed shape, but continued west as a 3000-mile horizontal stripe across the middle of North America, all the way to the Pacific.

The Ohio River Valley was the main prize on the minds of the warring countries, not only for its untapped natural resources, but for trade with the native tribes therein. But the "Doctrine of Discovery" under which both countries had staked their claims had an important corollary: in order to maintain the territorial rights that discovery of new lands conferred on the discoverer, the discoverer had to occupy the claimed territory.

The French, spurred by the indecisive outcome of the last war, and anxious to strengthen and expand their claims in the Mississippi Valley, decided to build a chain of forts throughout the Ohio Valley. From a military perspective, the most strategic area to secure was at the confluence of three rivers in Western Pennsylvania: the Ohio, the Allegheny, and the Monongahela. Incidentally, those same three rivers would later give a name to a baseball stadium at that spot: the Pirates' Three Rivers Stadium.

To establish these forts, the governor of New France sent one of his best officers, Captain Pierre-Joseph Celoron de Blainville. In 1749, the competent Celoron shepherded his small party in birchbark canoes on a remarkable 3,000 mile journey – from Montreal to upstate New York, down to Western Pennsylvania, finally to Ohio, then back to Montreal.[23] At six different locations along the way, he engaged in a solemn ceremony. With his troops arrayed in dress uniforms, Celoron read a proclamation reasserting French sovereignty in the territory. Then, with great pomp, he buried a lead plate bearing the heraldic arms of the King of France that recited the historical events and documents that had created French dominion over the land. This curious ceremony, the French believed, would reassert their superior claim to the Ohio Valley beyond any English quibbling.

As we have seen, under the laws of territory-grabbing in vogue at the time, bodies of waters, especially flowing ones, were significant. A nation that claimed to have discovered a river or stream could claim ownership of every tributary of water upstream and every speck of land whose water drained into that stream. Thus, Celoron chose to bury his

---

23. Celoron would not lose a single man on his remarkable journey, fifty years before Lewis and Clark, and with far less support, technology, and supplies.

plates at the mouth of various waterways: two on the Allegheny where it met large creeks, and the others at the Muskingum River, Wheeling Creek, the Kanawha, and the Miami River.

On his tour, Celoron encountered not only various Indian tribes as expected, but bands of English traders and settlers, whom he considered to be lawless trespassers. He sent them packing, but not before writing an indignant letter to be carried back by the English interlopers to the Governor of Pennsylvania.

The letter read:

Sir: -

Having been sent with a detachment into these quarters by Monsieur the Marquis de la Galissoniere, commandant general of New France, to reconcile among themselves certain savage nations, who are ever at variance on account of the war just terminated, I have been much surprised to find some traders of your government in a country to which England never had any pretensions. It even appears that the same opinion is entertained in New England, since in many of the villages I have passed through, the English who were trading there have mostly taken flight. Those whom I first fell in with, and by whom I write you, I have treated with all the mildness possible, although I would have been justified in treating them as interlopers and men without design, their enterprise being contrary to the preliminaries of peace signed five months ago. I hope, sir, you will carefully prohibit for the future this trade, which is contrary to treaties; and give notice to your traders that they will expose themselves to great risks in returning to these countries, and that they must impute only to themselves, the misfortunes they may meet with. I know that our commandant general would be very sorry to have recourse to violence, but he has orders not to permit foreign traders in his government.

I have honor to be with great respect, Sir your humble and obedient servant.

CELORON

In typical French fashion, the letter used language both polite and *diplomatique*, but made plain its message: this was French territory alone, and further trespasses would not be tolerated.

Celoron was of course wrong; the English did have more than "pretensions" to the Ohio Valley. And those competing claims would in fact spark the next war. This time, it would be known as the Seven Years' War, and on this continent, as the French and Indian War. Or, as taught in modern-day Quebec, *La guerre de la Conquête* – the War of the Conquest.

How did the War start?

Well, it took several years, but the English finally got around to reading Celoron's impudent letter. They responded with indignation, however tardy.

The person who took it upon himself to answer Celoron's shot across the bow was the lieutenant governor of Virginia, Robert Dinwiddie. He happened to be a shareholder in the "Ohio Company," a group of Virginia colonists with a speculative interest in the Ohio Valley. The Company had been granted 200,000 acres of prime land in Ohio by the British Crown. There was a catch, however: the grant required the Company to populate the land with one hundred families.

The French's creation of new forts in the territory alarmed Dinwiddie, who saw the prospective fortunes of his Ohio Company in peril. The French forts were a direct threat to possession of the lands that the King of England had granted to Dinwiddie's group. He badgered the Crown to respond with British outposts to counter the French expansion.

Eventually he won his point. King George II agreed to allow Dinwiddie to build the desired forts, at the Crown's expense, provided he try diplomacy first. Dinwiddie was instructed to provide the French with proofs of England's legal claim to the disputed territory. The French, if they sensibly acceded to Britain's clearly superior claims, were to be allowed to pull up stakes and run away, if they so chose. If not, Dinwiddie was authorized to build his forts and to "repel force with force."

So, in 1753, Dinwiddie wrote a letter rebutting the French's haughty claim to sole possession of the Ohio Valley. As he could not leave his post to deliver it in person, he put the letter in the hands of another shareholder of the Ohio Company to carry it to the French commander-in-chief. This would require a journey of several hundred miles, from the Virginia capital of Williamsburg, up to Alexandria, Virginia, then up the banks of the Potomac to the Cumberland Gap. The intended destination of the delegation was Venango, a former English trading post on the Allegheny River seized just months earlier by a French expedition and converted into a crude fort. There, they expected to find the French commander and hand him the English reply to Celoron's letter, almost four years later.

Along the way, the Virginia delegation called at an Indian settlement called Logstown to pay their respects to Tanaghrisson, the chief of the Seneca tribe. The French had established relationships with various Indian tribes, who had proved valuable allies in the past. The English needed to make Indian allies of their own if war were to break out in the disputed lands. Tanaghrisson, called "Half King" by the English, received the Virginians and their tribute of presents, especially their wampum belts, warmly. He even agreed to accompany the delegation to see the French, for added protection.

When the Virginia delegation arrived at Fort Venango, they were politely received by the French officer in charge, and told that the commander of the French forces, alas, was not at Venango, but at Fort LeBoeuf, several days' journey up French Creek, near Lake Erie. Determined to complete their mission, the Virginians tramped on to Fort LeBoeuf.

At LeBoeuf, the French commandant, Captain Jacques Legardeur de Saint Pierre, also politely received the English delegation and read Dinwiddie's letter. It recited the origins of England's rights to the Ohio

Valley, and commanded the French to peaceably depart in light of England's superior claim. Legardeur politely declined the suggestion. The Virginians departed to report back to Dinwiddie that the message had been delivered, and rejected.

As the King had commanded, Dinwiddie had tried diplomacy first, even if the attempt were perfunctory and its outcome foreordained. Now, with diplomacy having failed, it was time to respond in kind to the French program of fort-building. The first site for an English counter-fort had already been determined, a spot on the Ohio River that the Ohio Company had chosen earlier. The fort was to be named, in honor of the Prince of Wales and future King of England, Fort Prince George.

First, Dinwiddie sent ahead a party of pioneers to begin construction on the fort. He then assembled a group of about 150 militia to follow them and prevent the French from interfering in the construction. Lastly, he put in command of the expedition the same young man who had just delivered Dinwiddie's letter to Fort LeBoeuf. The tall Virginian, just 22 years old, with no military experience of any kind, was appointed to the position of lieutenant colonel of Virginia's militia. As he set off for the planned site of Fort Prince George, he could not have suspected that his actions would actually be the spark that would launch the Seven Years' War.

He and his troops arrived too late. The advance building party, less than 40 strong, had come upon the planned site in February 1754 and immediately begun work. But the French through their Indian scouts quickly got wind of the fort's construction and responded forcefully. They swiftly mustered a force of over 500 troops, consisting of French regulars, colonial militia, and Indian troops, and set out to put an end to the English venture.

When the French, commanded by Claude-Pierre Pécaudy de Contrecoeur, arrived at the half-built fort, the badly outnumbered advance party quickly exercised the better part of valor, and were allowed to leave unharmed. The French tore down the shoddy British beginnings, and began to construct their own, stronger fort at the same location. Contrecoeur named it after his superior, the governor-general of New France: Fort Duquesne. Fort Duquesne no longer exists, but in its place stands the city of Pittsburgh.

When the lieutenant colonel from Virginia arrived in the area of the fort with his militia, he learned of the surrender and destruction of Fort Prince George. But he believed that reinforcements were on their way to back him under the command of Colonel Fry, his superior. Rather than retreat back to Virginia to report, he decided to construct the new fort, not at the planned site at the three rivers, but about 40 miles further southeast, at a place called Great Meadows. It wasn't the fort they had planned, but it would have to do. He called it Fort Necessity.

From his Indian allies, the French commander Contrecoeur was aware of the arrival of the second body of Virginia militia, but was not certain of their intentions. To ascertain the Virginians' location and actions, he sent one of his subordinates, a French officer named Joseph Coulon de Villiers de Jumonville, with a small detachment of about 35 men. Jumonville's orders were to locate the trespassing Virginians and order them off the lands belonging to the French king. Like several of his predecessor officers in this back-and-forth, he carried with him an official legal document to be read in stern tones to the trespassers.

A seasoned scout and trader from Virginia, Christopher Gist, had a farm and trading post in the area between the two forts. When Jumonville and his troops passed by his post, Gist hurried to the barely-begun diggings at Fort Necessity to warn the Virginians of the presence of the Frenchmen. The lieutenant colonel of the Virginia militia was duly alarmed. He feared that the French intended to attack Fort Necessity as they had Fort Prince George. In reality, Jumonville's party of 35 men was far too small to mount an offensive attack against 150 troops; moreover, he had strict orders not to engage the English unless they attacked him.

Nonetheless, in the eyes of the lieutenant colonel, the threat was real. He therefore immediately sent eighty men off under Gist's leadership to intercept the French and prevent any attempt to interfere with the fort's construction. Mere hours after Gist had departed with half the troops, a messenger from Tanaghrisson, the Seneca chief, came running to Fort Necessity with news. The Half King's scouts had found Jumonville's force, and they were only five miles from the fort. The French were unaware of the location of the English.

The inexperienced lieutenant colonel may have hesitated, but not for long. His more experienced Indian ally, Tanaghrisson, argued vehemently in favor of an immediate strike. The surprise attack appeared essential. Half his troops were gone, in the wrong direction, and could not be summoned back in time. He was unsure of the size of the French party, but he had a single advantage: he knew where the French were, and the French didn't know where he was. While he had foolishly divided his force by sending off Gist's group, he still had the element of surprise.

He again divided his remaining force in half, leaving 40 men to guard the fort and leading the other 40 men, together with Half King and a dozen of his Mingos, to the French encampment. It took them all night, trailing the Indians through a hard rain in pitch blackness, to arrive upon the sleeping Frenchmen.

At Tanaghrisson's suggestion, the Mingos circled around their camp to cut off escape. Half of the Frenchmen were still asleep; some had just started to cook breakfast. The English and Indians crept up on the unsuspecting French, hiding behind rocks and trees, to surround the camp. What happened next is unclear. Either one of the Frenchmen fired into the woods upon hearing a noise, and the Virginians returned fire, or perhaps the Virginians opened fire without warning. But in the initial exchange, several Frenchmen fell dead, and the survivors, wounded and unwounded, took flight away from the gunfire. Unfortunately, they ran directly into the waiting Indians. The French then fled back into the Virginians. Surrounded, they surrendered, laying down their arms. The skirmish was likely over in less than five minutes.

Jumonville, the French commander, was wounded, but he summoned his dignity and explained that he was there, not to attack the new fort, but merely to deliver the legalistic summons to again warn the Englishmen that they were interlopers on French soil. He produced the letter and ordered one of his aides to translate it into English for the benefit of their attackers.

Apparently, the translation did not go well. No doubt the translator's concentration was not aided by the fact that, minutes earlier, the sleepy French had been ambushed without warning, or that several of the translator's comrades lay dead on the ground, with more wounded groaning in pain. In any event, the lieutenant colonel asked Jumonville for the letter; he couldn't read or speak French, but perhaps one of his men could make sense of it.

While he was perusing the letter, the Half King decided to end the negotiation. He came up behind the wounded French commander, and said to him, in French, "Thou are not yet dead, my father."

Then he buried his hatchet in Jumonville's head.

What followed next by Tanaghrisson was even worse. He reached into Jumonville's open skull, pulled out his brains and washed his hands with them.

Tanaghrisson's Mingo braves understood this as a signal for a general massacre. They fell upon the disarmed French with their knives and hatchets, slaughtering them and scalping the corpses.

It took some time for the stunned lieutenant colonel to comprehend what was happening and take steps to protect the French prisoners from the Indians. When he and his men finally regained control of the situation, and surveyed the scene, nearly a dozen Frenchman lay dead. One had already been decapitated, and his head put on a stake. The remaining twenty or so French prisoners cowered in shock behind the Virginia militiamen who protected them from Half King's Mingos.

The young commander was aghast at the barbarity of the massacre he had just witnessed. It was his first military action ever, and the first bloodshed in war he had ever seen. He had accepted the surrender of the French, but his Indian troops had disregarded that surrender and butchered half of them in cold blood.

Tanaghrisson, his supposed advisor and ally, had split open the skull of a French officer and, in a scene of unbelievable savagery, *bathed his hands in the man's brains.*

This was bad. Very bad. Even though he had played no part in the massacre, or had any forewarning about the Half King's penchant for open-air brain surgery, the Virginian knew that blame for it would fall not on the uncivilized Indians, but on the man in command: him. Worse than the damage to his reputation and career, this could be an international incident of grave consequence. The Ohio Valley was already a powderkeg with the French and English competing claims having evolved into the saber-rattling campaign of fort-building. The French would not respond well to the report that one of their officers, who had surrendered to an English commander, had had his head split with an axe, with the murderer defiling the corpse by rummaging in its brainpan for souvenirs. It was a violation of the rules of civilized war. Moreover, it was a desecration of a French officer's corpse. Wars had started for far, far less.

The lieutenant commander therefore took it upon himself to record a much-sanitized version of what had actually transpired. He wrote in his diary that night:

> We were advanced pretty near to them, as we thought, when they discovered us; whereupon I ordered my company to fire; mine was supported by that of Mr. [Wagner's], and my Company and his received the whole Fire of the French, during the greatest Part of the Action, which only lasted a Quarter of an Hour, before the Enemy was routed.
>
> We killed Mr. de Jumonville, the commander of that Party, as also nine others; we wounded one, and made Twenty-one Prisoners...

The account is purposefully brief and devoid of details. There is no mention of the manner of Jumonville's death, or of the other French deaths. No mention of the head on a stake. No explanation of how ten Frenchman were killed and only one wounded; in most 18th century battles, with inaccurate flintlock muskets as the combatants' main weapons, the ratio of wounded to killed would be reversed. The omission of these details makes the account read like all French casualties occurred in a couple of musket volleys. The official report to his commanders would repeat this intentionally vague summary.

The English attempt to whitewash the massacre was futile. There were scores of witnesses to the battle, including more than twenty French soldiers who survived. It was impossible that the French would not learn of the butchery of their officer and his troops.

Thus, in the middle of Pennsylvania, a skirmish, involving less than a hundred combatants, and the resulting massacre, became known as the Battle of Jumonville Glen. And it would prove to be the match that lit the fuse to the French and Indian War.

Shortly after the battle, Jumonville's brother, Louis Coulon de Villiers, arrived at Fort Duquesne with reinforcements from Canada. Outraged by the report of the massacre of his brother and his troops, he sought to exact swift retribution. He begged Contrecoeur to allow him to lead a punitive mission against the Virginians who had murdered his brother. Contrecoeur agreed.

The bad fortune of the Virginia expedition continued. A relief force of 200 militia was on its way from Alexandria to reinforce Fort Necessity, led by the regiment's commanding colonel, Joshua Fry. But less than a hundred miles from Fort Necessity, Fry fell off his horse, broke his neck, and died. The reinforcements reached Fort Necessity nonetheless, but now the weight of command of the entire regiment fell on the inexperienced lieutenant colonel.

Almost a month after his brother's murder, de Villiers set out from Fort Duquesne at the head of the largest force either side had ever assembled in the Ohio Valley: 600 troops, accompanied by another 100 Indian allies. After a one-week's march, they arrived at Fort Necessity, still under construction.

The modern reconstruction of Fort Necessity. *Photo by author.*

The Virginians marched out to meet them, only to fall back to the half-built fort in the face of the overwhelming firepower of the French. A heavy rain fell, and the deluge soaked the Virginians' gunpowder kegs, making their powder unusable. The French fusillade was unrelenting. The poorly designed fortifications proved to be little protection to the defenders, and they dropped like flies. Demoralized, some of the Virginians broke into the rum supply and got drunk.

What saved the English at Fort Necessity from utter annihilation was the mercy of the French commander. Even with the defenders unable to fire virtually a single shot in reply, de Villiers suspended his attack and offered them generous terms of surrender. It was a godsend to the beleaguered English.

The French commander drafted a document detailing the terms of the surrender for the English commanding officer to sign. It included a clause in which the signer admitted to the "assassination" of Jumonville. It is unclear whether the lieutenant colonel fully understood the import of the French document. One of his aides with moderate fluency in French was attempting to translate the rain-soaked document, its ink blotted and running, by candlelight, and all were exhausted. It is certainly possible that, given a choice to escape their inevitable doom if the battle continued, he would have signed almost anything put in front of him. In any event, he signed the capitulation as drafted. Then he, and what was left of the Virginia militia, limped home, dragging their many wounded.

Britain, alarmed by the defeat at Fort Necessity and the French boldness in Ohio in general, organized an immediate escalation of hostilities. When the Crown received Dinwiddie's report of the Fort Necessity debacle, plans were immediately made to respond in force. Two regiments of troops, under the command of an irascible and incompetent general named Braddock, sailed from England to attack French holdings in the Ohio Valley and erase the humiliation of Fort Necessity.

The French, armed with the propaganda of the Fort Necessity surrender agreement, also had their *casus belli*. The English had admitted, in writing, to the murder of Jumonville. He must be avenged. French spies almost immediately learned of the planned British expedition under Braddock, and the French countered, with three thousand French soldiers setting sail from France for Canada. War had begun.

Braddock landed at Alexandria, Virginia and lingered there for some weeks, collecting supplies and recruiting additional troops from the colonists. Then, with a force of about 2,200 men, he marched up to the Cumberland Gap, hoping to repay the disaster of Fort Necessity by taking Fort Duquesne. On Braddock's staff was the same Virginian lieutenant colonel of militia who had presided over the debacle at Fort Necessity and signed the capitulation admitting to Jumonville's assassination.

As the British approached Fort Duquesne, a mixed force of French and Indians moved outside the fort to set an ambush. They intercepted

Braddock's force a few miles outside the fort and utterly destroyed it. Braddock was mortally wounded and died a few days later on the headlong retreat of the defeated British back to Alexandria.

The murder of Jumonville in a wooded glen would lead to a war that would be fought in North America, Europe, Africa, India, and the Caribbean. It would be the first true "world war," and would lead to hundreds of thousands of deaths, perhaps as many as a million.

It would also lead to the end of French rule in Canada. After early French victories, the English responded by pouring tens of thousands of troops into the North American woods. They sought to not only regain the Ohio Valley territory the French had occupied, but to pursue the French back into their home, their settlements in Canada. In 1759, one by one, the French bases fell, including Quebec City.

Only Montreal held out, but it could not last against the overwhelming British forces. In September 1760, the governor of New France surrendered Montreal to the British commander, Major General Jeffrey Amherst. The war would drag on another two years elsewhere, but Canada was British territory, for good.

It had all started at Jumonville Glen. The British parliamentarian and historian, Horace Walpole, summed up the effect of the tiny skirmish in Pennsylvania. "The volley fired by a young Virginian in the backwoods of America set the world on fire." He was right.

So, who was this "young Virginian"? Who was this inexperienced lieutenant colonel who fired the volley, which caused the Seven Years' War, which caused the British to rule Canada, which caused the French-Canadians to seethe for 250 years, which caused them to pass Bill 101, which caused the Expos to die, which caused them to move to Washington and become the Nationals?

His name was George Washington.

CHAPTER 12

The Father of the Curse

GEORGE WASHINGTON.

The Father of his Country. The man in command at Jumonville Glen, whose troops savagely butchered Joseph Coulon de Villiers de Jumonville, became the first President of the United States. I bet you never heard that story when they were talking about George Washington in elementary school, did you? It doesn't fit in with the boy who cannot tell a lie, or who crossed the Delaware on Christmas night to win the Battle of Trenton, does it?

George Washington. As in the Washington Monument.

As in Washington, DC.

The home of the Washington Nationals.

We've found it. We've found the Origin of the Curse. Ground Zero.

Ensign Jumonville, a soldier from Montreal, had surrendered to Lt. Colonel George Washington. Under the rules of war, he and his troops were prisoners, entitled to the protection and safekeeping of Washington, the commanding officer. But Washington allowed his Indian friend Tanaghrisson to perform a brainectomy on Jumonville and slaughter a dozen or more of his fellow unarmed Frenchmen.

That massacre was the direct cause of the French and Indian War. Twenty years later, that same Virginian lieutenant colonel became commander in chief of the entire American rebel army, and would eventually lead them to defeat the British and win independence for the colonies.

That same lieutenant colonel became the first President of the newly formed United States of America. The United States of America created a new capital city – one that had never existed before – and named it after that lieutenant colonel who murdered Jumonville.

Two hundred years later, that same city gets a baseball team. The team moves from Jumonville's hometown of Montreal to the city named for the man responsible for Jumonville's murder. *Of course* that team is going to be cursed.

This is, as far as I know, the only sports curse involving a murder. Unlike the Curse of the Bambino, or some incident involving disrespect to a barnyard animal, or Colonel Sanders, we are dealing with some serious juju here. This isn't trading a human being to another team. This is killing a human being, then bathing in his brains.

Clearly, the ghost of Jumonville has had his revenge. That murder and desecration has led to the Nationals' years of misery. Max's Inning from Hell wasn't Max's fault, or his catcher's fault, or the umpiring crew's – it was Jumonville's vengeance on George Washington and his city's baseball team.

Why does Jumonville reach from the spirit world, over 250 years later, to haunt the hopes of the Nationals? Part of the power of the Curse lies in its heinousness. Curses involving murder are the most potent curses in history and literature. Remember Tantalus? The man who served his son up as a meal for the gods? Tantalus is the archetype of the Curse of the Nationals. He was doomed to spend eternity perpetually hungry and thirsty, with food and drink just inches out of his reach. Likewise, the Nationals and their fans are doomed to spend eternity perpetually hungry for that World Series ring, with victory suspended just out of their grasp.

Jumonville's murder was doubly heinous. As brutal as war can be, the persons of prisoners of war have been considered inviolate for centuries. The prohibition against killing them can be found as far back as the Old Testament:

> And the king of Israel said unto Elisha, when he saw them, My father, shall I smite them? shall I smite them? And he answered, Thou shalt not smite them: wouldest thou smite those whom thou hast taken captive with thy sword and with thy bow? set

bread and water before them, that they may eat and drink, and go to their master. And he prepared great provision for them: and when they had eaten and drunk, he sent them away, and they went to their master. So the bands of Syria came no more into the land of Israel.[24]

In particular, the European nations prided themselves on conducting war honorably, as gentlemen would. For example, a captured officer could merely give his parole, his promise not to fight again (until given permission by an agreed exchange of officers), and he would be released to go home, on the universal expectation that he would keep his word. While the rules of war in 1754 may not have been reduced to writing or formalized in a treaty, they nonetheless formed a code of honor held in common between the French and English. And one of the agreed principles was that a surrendering soldier not only could not be killed, but the officer accepting his surrender in essence became responsible for his safety.

Washington, as green a commander as he would have been in 1754, would absolutely have known the prohibition against slaughtering surrendering troops. His inartful efforts to whitewash the Jumonville affair in his journal and official documents reflect an awareness of the gravity of the offense. His later writings also confirm this knowledge. In the American Revolution in 1775, he sent the infamous Benedict Arnold (then an American military hero, not yet a traitor) to attack Quebec. In Washington's written orders to Arnold, he included this specific command:

> Any Prisoners who may fall into your Hands, you will treat with as much Humanity and kindness, as may be consistent with your own Safety and the publick Interest. Be very particular in restraining not only your own Troops, but the Indians from all

---

24. 2 Kings 6:21-23 (KJV).

Acts of Cruelty and Insult, which will disgrace the American Arms, and irritate our Fellow Subjects against us.

It is clear that the shadow of what befell in Jumonville Glen still haunted Washington in 1775.

The plaque commemorating the skirmish at Jumonville Glen. Like Washington's journal, unsavory details of Jumonville's death have been omitted. *Photo by author.*

Yet the murder of Jumonville was an even greater outrage, because he was not even acting in a military role. The French contended that

Jumonville's mission was to seek out the English and read them the French's formal protest of their presence in the Ohio Valley – just as George Washington had delivered a similar document to the French commander at Fort LeBoeuf the year before. He was therefore engaged, not in a military mission, but on a diplomatic mission. As such, according to the French, he was acting as a *de facto* ambassador, entitled to the same deference and protections as any other diplomat.

In other words, the entire expedition, in French eyes, was being conducted under a flag of truce. Its only purpose was to deliver the summons of protest. If true, Washington had no right to attack Jumonville's force at all. Indeed, according to the most detailed account of that day, Jumonville was in the midst of performing his diplomatic assignment --- having his official summons read to the English --- when Tanaghrisson buried his hatchet in his head.[25]

---

25. In his journal, in contrast to the extremely sparse description of the actual battle, Washington spends a great deal of time trying to undermine the French claims of a diplomatic mission. The entire entry smacks more of a man trying to "paper over" a grave breach of the rules of war, than of a man later revered for his honesty.

> *[The French prisoners] informed me that they had been sent with a Summons to order me to depart.* A plausible Pretence to discover our camp, and to obtain the Knowledge of our Forces and Situation! It was so clear that they were come to reconnoiter what we were, that I admired at their Assurance, when they told me they were come as an Embassy...And instead of coming as an Embassadore, publickly, and in an open manner, they came secretly, and sought after the most hidden Retreats, more like Deserters than Embassadors....Besides, an Embassador has princely Attendants; whereas this was only a simple petty *French* Officer; an Embassador has no Need of Spies.

The entry continues in this vein for several paragraphs, espousing rambling and sometimes contradictory arguments to excuse his conduct. He argues, for example that the summons Jumonville carried was insulting, and also that if he had not attacked the French, his Indian allies would have abandoned him. Obviously, neither of these, even if true, would excuse the ambush of a diplomatic mission.

Despite Washington's protestations, both the size of Jumonville's force and his orders from his superiors confirm the exploratory and diplomatic character of the expedition. Contrecoeur knew from his scouts that Washington had almost 200 men, with more reinforcements rumored. Sending a detachment of 35 soldiers to attack a force more than five times larger would be suicidal folly.

Washington thus committed multiple violations of the rules of war. The first was that the two countries, despite the last few years of saber-rattling in the Ohio Valley, weren't at war, giving Washington no excuse for the unprovoked ambush. The second was that he attacked a diplomatic party; the third, after the party had surrendered, he allowed the murder of a dozen of the prisoners.

The worst by far, and the sin that caused the Nationals' woes, was the desecration of Jumonville's body. The violation of a dead body has been, since time immemorial, one of the most heinous acts in civilized society. Homer's *Iliad*, one of the oldest foundational texts of Western culture, contains this moral lesson. The Greek hero Achilles, in rage over the death of his friend Patroclus, kills the Trojan Hector. He refuses to surrender his body to the Trojans for burial, and instead drags the body around the city of Troy behind his chariot. Zeus, the king of the Olympian gods, is displeased by this outrage and must intervene to remind Achilles of his obligation to respect the dead. The chastened Achilles relents and sends the body back to Hector's father. The burial of Hector with full honors is the final scene in the epic poem.

Tanaghrisson's bathing in Jumonville's brains is about as heinous as it gets. Washington knew, as a good Anglican, that the mutilation of Jumonville was also a sin in the Christian faith. He believed, as did the Catholic Jumonville, that when Christ returned, all true Christians would be resurrected in their physical bodies. Thus, the body must be preserved intact. This belief led to religious prohibitions against cremation, for example, and laws in England forbidding the dissection of corpses by medical men.

Tanaghrisson's playing with Jumonville's cerebrum like Play-Doh viciously broke that taboo. When Washington and his troops departed, leaving Jumonville literally lying in pieces on the ground of that clearing in Pennsylvania, a sacrilege had been committed. Today the Nats and their fans continue to pay the price for that sacrilege.

Jumonville's Curse is not the first of its kind. Dead bodies are not to be disturbed. Those that are have responded with some of the most famous curses in history.

In 1922, the British archaeologist Howard Carter opened the tomb of the pharaoh Tutankhamun. Within five month of the tomb's opening, the sponsor of Carter's expedition, Lord Carnavon, who was present at the tomb's opening, died of an infected insect bite. Within a year, other participants in the expedition died suddenly: one of a fever; one was shot dead by his wife; another died of an unknown illness.

Other associates and relatives of Carter or Carnavon dropped like flies in the next decade. A member of the excavation team died from arsenic poisoning. Another went blind. Carnarvon's brother died from malaria. Carter's personal secretary was smothered to death, then the secretary's father committed suicide.

Thus was born the Curse of Tutankhamun, caused by the sacrilege of failing to respect the peace of the pharaoh's burial.

Then there's the curse of Tamurlane. Tamurlane, also known as Timur, was the last great Mongol conqueror. Claiming the mantle of his hero, Genghis Khan, Tamurlane ruthlessly conquered almost all of Central Asia, from Turkey to Pakistan, and up to Russia in the north. In the course of his campaigns in the latter part of the 14th century, he is supposed to be responsible for the deaths of about one-twentieth of the entire world's population at that time.

Tamurlane was buried in a distinctive mausoleum in Samarkand, Uzbekistan. You would think that people would leave a man like that alone. Yet, in June 1941, in the middle of World War II, the Soviets dug him up for scientific and historical research.

Things had been going well for the Soviets at that time. Their ally Germany had destroyed the armies of Poland, France and Belgium with ease, and was on the verge of invading Britain. The Russian armies were having similar successes, invading the Baltic States and Eastern Europe from the east. The USSR and Germany seemed on the brink of dividing control of Europe between them.

But the Russians soon learned that disturbing Tamurlane's eternal rest had consequences. Three days after the opening of Tamurlane's tomb, Hitler treacherously renounced the alliance with the Russians and launched Operation Barbarossa, the invasion of Russia. It was the largest invasion force ever assembled in history: almost four million Axis troops and over three thousand tanks.

Germany's invasion of Russia would lead directly to a staggering five million Russian casualties over the next two years. All because the Russians wouldn't leave a dead man alone.

Then there's Ötzi the Iceman. In 1991, two hikers in the Ötztal Alps in Austria saw a body lying in a crevasse, which they believed to be another modern hiker who had fallen to his death. When the authorities came to retrieve the body, they discovered that it was not a careless hiker, but a careless warrior from the Copper Age, 5000 years ago. An arrowhead in his shoulder suggested he was the victim of a skirmish with an enemy tribe. His corpse had been so well protected by the ice, cold, and altitude of the Alps that scientists were able to study perfectly preserved clothes and tools, and even discern his last meal (ibex, red deer, and bread).

Again, Ötzi didn't appreciate his rescue from his icy grave, and took it out on those who had disturbed his rest. Helmut Simon, one of the hikers who found Ötzi, failed to return from a mountain hike and was found dead. Like his famous find, he was found frozen, under a sheet of snow and ice. He had apparently fallen to his death. Konrad Spindler, head of the Iceman investigation team at Innsbruck University that had examined Ötzi, died suddenly in 2005, from complications caused by multiple sclerosis.

Dr. Rainer Henn, a medical examiner who actually handled the body, died in an automobile accident on his way to a conference. The conference's topic was – what else? – Ötzi. The mountain guide who supervised Ötzi's removal by helicopter was killed by a snowslide in the mountains. Rainer Hoelz, a journalist present at the recovery of the Iceman, developed a brain tumor and passed away.

These curses stemmed from merely disturbing the rest of a dead body. How about Tanaghrisson's desecration of Jumonville's still-warm corpse?

We know that Washington understood the principle of respect for the dead, and thus fully grasped the barbarity of Tanaghrisson's act. The best evidence we have of Washington's views is how he treated the body of his commanding officer, General Braddock. When Braddock died from his wounds on the retreat from his disastrous expedition against Fort Duquesne, Washington personally made sure that Braddock's body would not be subject to similar defilement. In order that the pursuing Indians allied to the French would not treat Braddock's body as his own Indian allies had treated Jumonville's, Washington took great pains to hide Braddock's burial site. Braddock was buried in the middle of the road leading back to Virginia; then all the retreating troops were ordered to march over the grave. When they were done, the foottreads of hundreds of British soldiers had removed any clue of the location of the freshly dug grave.

The final confirmation of the Curse comes from Tanaghrisson himself. In October 1754, less than five months after the murder, the Half King, the man who sank his axe into Jumonville's head and squeezed his brains between his hands, suddenly died. He had not been ill, and his death came without any warning. According to his tribe, the cause of his unexpected death was clear: a curse had been placed on him.

Just like the Nationals die every October, from the same curse.

CHAPTER 13

Expiation

WE HAVE DETERMINED THAT THE Curse was founded in 1754 in the clearing at Jumonville Glen. That is important, but merely the first step. The far more pressing issue for Nats fan is a practical one. How is such a curse removed?

The Red Sox and their fans tried for years to exorcise the Curse of the Bambino. Most of their efforts were lighthearted stunts, like asking a fake priest from Saturday Night Live to bless the team. But in 1999, before Game 5 of the 1999 ALCS, they trotted out the big gun: they asked the daughter of Babe Ruth, Julia Ruth Stevens, to throw out the first pitch. It didn't work.

The Cubs tried to atone as well. They brought in a descendant of Murphy, the offended billy goat, led by Sam Sianis, the nephew of the offended owner of the billy goat. They had a Greek Orthodox priest come and bless the Cub dugout one preseason. (A nice touch – if anyone can lift a Greek's curse, it's a Greek priest.) Later, a Chicago restaurant owned by Cubs announcer Harry Caray bought the infamous "Bartman ball" – the ball Steve Bartman had interfered with – and in 2004 had it publicly destroyed in an elaborate ritual. It got the chair. The ball was "electrocuted." Not to leave any residue of the ball's magic power, its ashes were ground up, made into spaghetti sauce, and dished out to the Cubs faithful. If that was the cure, it sure took its time – the Cubs would not win the Series for another twelve years.

But how are curses expiated, when the curse involves the butchery of a French soldier 250 years ago? The origins of the other baseball curses are frivolous by comparison with the Nats'. Expelling an unwelcome pet goat from a game? Dunking a statue of the founder of a fast food chain? Selling a player, even the greatest player ever in the history of the game? None of these was marked by blood. None of these involved the actual murder of a human being. If selling Babe Ruth can lead to eight decades of misery for the Red Sox, how many centuries will the Nationals suffer as a result the savage butchery of Jumonville by Tanaghrisson?

On a cool day in June, I decided to visit the site of the origin of the Curse. Fort Necessity is a national historic site, and it's only about a 200-mile drive from Nationals Park. I thought that maybe communing with the spirits of Jumonville Glen might give some hint of how to exorcise the Nationals' Curse.

First, I paid my respects at the park itself, where a reproduction of Washington's primitive fort has been erected to commemorate that disastrous battle. Then I drove northwest from Fort Necessity, in the same direction that Tanaghrisson's Mingos had led Washington the night of May 28. The site of the battle of Jumonville Glen is not particularly well marked. Nor is the scene upon arrival particularly remarkable – just a parking lot and a small wooden building.

On this day, I had the site of the Curse largely to myself. To arrive at the precise birthplace of the Nationals' Curse, one must follow a roughly oval-shaped trail that meanders down to where the ambush occurred. If you walk the trail counterclockwise from the parking lot, you arrive first at the rock outcropping where Washington sprung his ambush.

There has been no real change in the topography of Jumonville Glen since that day in 1754. The small clearing where the French camped is still there, as is the short cliff overhanging the clearing, from which Washington launched his surprise attack. Once there, it is not hard to recreate the battle in your mind. The French, seeking shelter from the rainy night, constructing makeshift lean-tos in the lee of the cliff; the Virginians, arriving shortly before dawn, creeping quietly up behind

Jumonville Glen's marker. The site of the massacre is about a seven mile drive northwest of the Fort Necessity site. *Photo by author.*

the rocks and boulders atop the cliff, while Tanaghrisson's band circled around to cut off escape.

As the French soldiers were beginning to rise, collecting gear, making fires, or relieving their bladders, the opening volley from the Virginians would have been fired almost straight down, from near perfect cover, from a distance of a mere ten yards. Then a second group of Virginians hidden in the woods to Washington's right unleashed a second volley. One can imagine two or three men, hit by musket fire, crying out in pain, with equally panicked yells from the unwounded, while Jumonville screamed out orders, attempting to rally his stunned troops. But the overwhelming impulse for all would have been to snatch up their weapons and flee from the direction of the musket fire, gaining distance from the attackers in order to regroup and return fire. When they did, the French ran directly into the waiting Indians and their tomahawks. They turned and fled back into the clearing, and surrender was the only option. They threw down their arms, and minutes later came Jumonville's grisly death at the hands of the Half King. With it, the Curse of the Nationals was born.

The site of the Curse's birth. Washington's party would have been on the top of the little cliff, firing straight down on Jumonville's unsuspecting party below, from a distance shorter than from the mound to home plate. *Photo by author.*

The clearing where Tanaghrisson butchered Ensign Jumonville, looking down from atop the cliff. *Photo by author.*

Washington's journal doesn't really tell us the full extent of what happened to Jumonville's corpse. Did Washington try to alleviate the barbarity of the slaughter by burying the French, or out of respect permit the French prisoners to do so? In his diary on the evening after the battle, Washington recorded:

> The Indians scalped the Dead, and took away the most Part of their arms, after which we marched on with the Prisoners and the Guard, to the Indian Camp, where again I held a Council with the Half-King .... After this I marched on with the Prisoners.

So while Washington admits that the French dead were scalped by the Mingos, he is silent about any burial of Jumonville and the other fallen

French. But one of the other accounts of the battle of Jumonville Glen, given by an English soldier named John Shaw, is quite clear that the bodies of the dead Frenchmen were not buried.

Even without Shaw's testimony, it would seem a safe assumption that the dead were left unburied. Washington and his troops would have been exhausted from the all-night march of the previous night from Fort Necessity to Jumonville's camp. They could easily have been suffering from a form of post-traumatic stress disorder from the gruesome acts they had witnessed. It is perhaps understandable that Washington didn't take the time to dig a dozen French graves – he may not even have had the proper tools. In any event, it is almost certain that Jumonville and his fellow dead Frenchmen were left where they lay, to become food for carrion.

Serious curses call for serious acts of atonement. So then, how can George Washington's sin be put aright? How do we lay to rest the ghost of Ensign Jumonville?

Fortunately, there is a textbook for the removal of curses. James Frazer's masterful work, *The Golden Bough,* is a survey of the world's beliefs of religion and magic. The twelve-volume set, which took Frazer over 25 years to write, is one of the greatest works of anthropology in history, and it contains an encyclopedic recital of the beliefs in curses, ghosts, and taboos of virtually every culture in the world.

In this situation, where a curse has been placed due to a homicide, or by a vengeful ghost, there are several options for its removal, as catalogued by Frazer. One is the ritual purification of the killer. If the killer undergoes certain acts of atonement, such as a temporary exile from the community or eating only certain foods, the ghost of the slain is appeased, and any hex is averted. Obviously, that's not an option here: George is not available to undergo any purging rituals.

Wait a second. George's replica is here – in the form of one of the Racing Presidents. If we can't purify George through exile from the community, we could exile George's stand-in. What if we banish Mascot George from any future races for his transgression? As described by

Frazer, the killer's purification-by-isolation isn't permanent – just a temporary quarantine. Would a one-year ban from the Presidents' Race be sufficient to assuage Jumonville's wrath? (At a minimum, George definitely shouldn't be winning any races for the next several years. He'll survive – Teddy did.)

Another curse-averting option is to change the name of the killer. The idea is that if the killer is not mentioned by his correct name, then the avenging ghost is confused, and doesn't know where to direct his vengeance. That might work here. All we need to do is to change the name of the team. No more "Washington Nationals" – from henceforth, the "District of Columbia Nationals." It doesn't exactly roll off the tongue, but it would remove the name of Jumonville's enemy from the team. It's a small price to pay if it will get the Nats to the World Series. Or you could move the team across the Potomac to Arlington – Jumonville will never find them there.

A third possible cure for curses is to provide a sacrificial offering to pacify the ghost. There are many forms the sacrifice can take, from gifts of food, to games in honor of the dead, to actual sacrifices of animals and even humans. Would an offering to Ensign Jumonville's unquiet spirit be in order?

One possible such offering would be to pay homage to the Nationals' Canadian heritage. From day one, the Nats' ownership made it clear that they wanted to make a clean break with any Expos history. They wanted the Nationals to give the appearance of a shiny, brand-new franchise. Other than the names of a few famous Expos gracing the upper decks at Nationals Park, there is very little to remind the fans that this team used to reside in Montreal.

In Nationals Park, there are statues of Walter Johnson and Frank Howard, both Senators, and even one of Josh Gibson, from the Homestead Grays of the Negro leagues. There are zero Expos with a statue. There are three "pennants" flying out above the centerfield Jumbotron, bearing the years 1924, 1925, and 1933. Those pennants belong to the original Washington Senators, not the Nationals. They need to be packed up and shipped to Minnesota, where, I am sure, the Senators, now playing as the Minnesota Twins, would appreciate their return. Even the Nats announcers and PR department get in on the erasure of the Expos – when they talk about a player setting a "team record," when what they usually mean is a *Nationals* record, i.e., since 2005 when the franchise moved to D.C.

Was that rejection of the Nationals' Canadian past a mistake? The Expos version of this franchise has far more to be proud about than the Nationals iteration--- such as a half dozen Hall of Famers, including three who went in as Expos. Of the top ten players in franchise history by WAR, seven are Expos. A number of the franchise records set by Expos will likely never be broken: stolen bases (Raines, 635), OPS (Guerrero, .978), wins (Rogers, 158), to name but a few. There's a great deal to embrace, and the Washington Nationals have, for reasons best known to their ownership, abandoned this history almost completely.

There are numerous other underacknowledged connections of the modern version of the Nationals to the Montreal Expos. Manager Davey Martinez played 431 games as an Expo, and put up some decent numbers (except as a pitcher: ERA of 54.00 as an Expo.) Third base coach Bob Henley is an Expo lifer: after spending his entire playing career in the Expos organization, he's entering his 17th year as one of its coaches. MASN color commentator F.P. Santangelo got his start with the Expos, and reminisces frequently on air about his four years in Montreal. We've seen that former skipper Dusty Baker played in the Blue Monday game, albeit as a Dodger.

Would a greater acknowledgment of the team's Montreal heritage suffice to remove the Curse? Who knows? It couldn't hurt.

For example, they could serve poutine or Montreal bagels at the concession stand. How about establishing a radio broadcast *en Francais*? How about some Expos jerseys as throwbacks? Heck, the Expos played 20 games in Puerto Rico in 2004. How about a few Nationals home games in Olympic Stadium? A Vlad Guerrero bobblehead? Rusty Staub left us last fall for the great Hall of Fame in the sky, but there are lots of Expos around to throw out a first pitch. Steve Rogers, anyone?

I know: "The Happy Wanderer." It's that song that everyone used to know from summer camp or something, with the chorus, "Valdaree! Valdarah! Valdaree! Valdara-ha-ha-ha-ha-ha!" It was the Expos' theme song, played by their organist incessantly – before the game, during the game, after the game. What if, as a tribute to the Montreal days, the Nationals adopted it as their seventh-inning stretch song? Beats the heck out of "Take on Me." Would that help to slay the Curse?

Or perhaps a different offering to Jumonville's ghost. Maybe he would be placated by a new Montreal major league baseball team to replace the Expos. It's not a ridiculous thought --- it could actually happen. When I toured Olympic Stadium last year, our guide, who had spent his childhood attending dozens of Expos games each summer, waxed evangelical over the possibility of baseball's return to Montreal. He even pulled out his iPad to show me the new proposed plans for a baseball-only stadium. Lest you think him overexuberant, MLB has indeed discussed the potential expansion to 32 teams, with Montreal, together with Mexico City, mentioned as frontrunners for the two new slots.

Or do we need to recreate the sacrificial scene of Jumonville Glen, only in reverse? The expiation of curses caused by the shedding of blood sometimes require the shedding of more blood in repayment. Imagine it's Opening Day. From the Nationals dugout comes Screech, hand/wings bound behind him. From the visitors' dugout emerges Youppi!, armed with a Louisville Slugger (a Rusty Staub signed version, if possible.) On the pitcher's mound, Screech kneels. After a period of Youppi! gesticulating, and Screech pleading (these are mascots after all – they're not allowed to talk), Youppi! splits Screech's head with the baseball bat. Stuffing spills freely from the opening in Screech's head. As mothers hide their children's eyes, Youppi! reaches into the gaping wound in Screech's plush head, pulls out the cotton wool and *washes his hands in the stuffing.*

Would that do it? I don't know. I doubt the Lerners would let us try. Moreover, as much as the ritual sacrifice of Screech might be pleasing to some, I don't think it would appease Jumonville's ghost. It might worsen the Curse – he might rightly view the play-acting by giant fuzzy puppets, however well-intended, as making light of the grave injustice of his death.

To fully undertake the expiation of the Curse of the Nationals, we must fully address its nature. We have seen how the Curse has revealed itself, first in Montreal, but later, even more heartbreakingly in Washington. But those are merely the Curse's manifestations, not its cause. The clues to removing the Curse are not to be found in Max's Inning from Hell, or even in the misery of Blue Monday. To stand any chance of exorcising the ghost of Monsieur Jumonville, we must look to the root: the deeds at Jumonville Glen.

What, therefore, is the essence of the original sin that George Washington committed that day in 1754?

Jumonville's body lay, unburied, in the clearing that now bears his name. It took more than a month for his brother to arrive in the area to avenge his death on Washington at Fort Necessity. If his brother had chanced upon the site of the attack, there would be nothing of Jumonville left to bury. Buzzards and crows, opossums and foxes, and soon maggots and worms would have each had their turns on the corpse. Even the bones would have been stolen by opportunistic predators for later consumption. Likely, no more than a faded, tattered uniform marked the spot where the ensign had fallen, the rest either decayed or devoured.

As noted previously, Tanaghrisson's horrifying act of defilement is a taboo in virtually any civilized culture. But it was especially a desecration in the Catholicism of the 18th century that Jumonville would have devoutly believed. A Catholic's dread was to die "unshriven," without a priest to hear his last confession and to administer the last rites of extreme unction. Not only did Jumonville suffer this terrible fate, but even worse, he would have had no earthly body to resurrect at the Day of Judgment, and therefore barred from being part of the glories of eternal life.

To placate the ghost of Jumonville would seem to require the correction of this plight. The single best remedy to undo the Curse lies --- where else --- in Canada. So I went to Montreal to find out where Jumonville must be returned.

Jumonville grew up in a small village on the banks of the St. Lawrence, a few miles downstream from Montreal, called Verchères. Indeed, Jumonville's family was in essence the "first family" of Verchères. His aunt, Madeleine Jarret de Verchères, was a local hero, Verchères's version of Joan of Arc. Madeleine was born in 1678 at Verchères, the eldest of several Jarret children. Her parents had emigrated from France to become the founders of Verchères, at a time when the Iroquois were habitually on the warpath.

Her parents and others had built a small stockade at Verchères against the Indian raids. One day in October 1692, the parents and other adults left the stockade to gather supplies, leaving the 14-year-old Madeleine in charge. While she was tending to the fort's garden, the Iroquois suddenly attacked, and Madeleine hustled her brothers and sisters into the fort and barred the gate. Then with only two soldiers, one elderly man, and two younger brothers as her troops, she defended the fort against repeated Iroquois attacks. She held out for a week, until relieved by a force of Canadian settlers, collapsing into the arms of her rescuers.

The Catholic church in Verchères, *Église de Saint-François-Xavier*, was established in 1709. A small chapel was built in 1710, followed by a small church erected in 1724. Construction began on a second, larger church building in 1787. None of these buildings have survived to the present day. When the second church was destroyed in a fire in 1808, the current church was built in its place.

While *Saint-François-Xavier* has existed in several iterations, there is little doubt that it would have been the family church of the de Villiers. When Jumonville was born in Verchères in 1718, he would likely have

The church at Verchères, *Église de Saint-François-Xavier*. Jumonville would not have known this version, which was built over fifty years after his death. (*Photo credit: V.G. Bledsoe.*)

been christened in the first chapel of *Saint-François-Xavier*. He would have taken communion in the small church that replaced it. And if he had died in Verchères at a ripe old age, he would have been buried there, in its graveyard.

As I noted, no church or chapel from Jumonville's time remains. But the graveyard for *Saint-François-Xavier* is less than a mile upriver from the church itself. Verchères is a small community and thus has a modest cemetery; many of the gravestones and monuments date back more than a century.

It is to this graveyard that Jumonville needs to be returned. If such cannot be accomplished literally, perhaps it can be done figuratively. Jumonville's body was, quite literally, scattered throughout the forest at Jumonville Glen. His atoms and his molecules entered the ecosystem of the forest through the indignity of being eaten by its wildlife and dissolved by its natural processes. We can return Jumonville to Verchères by returning the only remaining remnants we have of him: the earth of Jumonville Glen.

The cemetery at Verchères, where Jumonville belongs. (*Photo credit: V.G. Bledsoe.*)

Ideally, one would fill a coffin with enough of the dirt of the clearing at Jumonville Glen to represent an 18th century Frenchman – say 150 pounds or so. This coffin could then be buried in the graveyard at Verchères.

The cemetery at Verchères. (*Photo credit: V.G. Bledsoe.*)

Unfortunately, it is probably too much to ask of the Catholic fathers at *Saint-François-Xavier* to permit a coffin of dirt to be buried in the holy ground of their cemetery. I doubt that they would see a casket filled with Pennsylvania soil as a proper recipient of the rite of Christian burial, however well intentioned.

An alternative plan could be to return Jumonville to Verchères, even though unsanctioned by the Church. A dedicated Cursebreaker might still find a way to put a bodyweight of Jumonville's dirt in a coffin, or any suitable receptacle, and deposit the dirt in Verchères. It need not go in the cemetery; in fact, the current cemetery was not in use in Jumonville's day. Perhaps Jumonville's spirit would be assuaged merely by the return of his "earthly" remains to his native village.

Nonetheless, dignity and respect for the corpse, or what we are substituting for the corpse, would need to be rigorously maintained. It's not a prank or a scavenger hunt. This is the ritual of burial that Jumonville never got, not a fraternity roadtrip. We would be conveying

Jumonville's dead body, or a facsimile thereof, to the proper interment that Washington denied the fallen Frenchman. That disrespect for the dead has earned the Nationals 50 years of failure---imagine what would happen if a careless fan were to redouble Jumonville's curse with further insult to his memory. The mind shudders in contemplation of it.

Even if we can't return Jumonville's earthly remains to Verchères, there are other things that can be done, under the Catholic faith, to ease a soul's experience in the afterlife. The Church has special rituals for circumstances where a believer has died but there is no corpse to bury, such as sailors lost at sea. In the absence of a body, the Church allows a memorial Mass in lieu of the funeral rite. A memorial Mass being said for Jumonville in Verchères, at his own family's church, would be particularly a nice touch.

Catholics believe that a soul's time in purgatory can be shortened by acts here on earth. Mere prayer helps, but having a Mass said specifically for a particular dead Catholic, known as the Mass for the repose of souls, is the heavy hitter. The church of St. Vincent DePaul, a couple of blocks from Nationals Park, offers a "Nationals Mass" every home Sunday at 12 noon. Perhaps if the priests there could include Ensign Jumonville in a Mass, that would shave something off the Curse.

The savage butchery of Ensign Jumonville cannot be undone. It may have been Washington's ally, rather than Washington, that struck the blow that started the Curse; still, it is Washington's fans who now are paying the toll. Perhaps through one of these suggestions, or some combination thereof, the spirit of Jumonville may be mollified, and the Nationals allowed to win a World Series.

The question is not whether there is a Nationals Curse – the question is why is no one talking about it?

I had recognized the Curse long before Max's Inning from Hell. When he took the mound on that Black Thursday to close out the Cubs, I genuinely knew in my heart that the Nats were doomed once again. There was no doubt about it. The scene was too perfect. The stars were

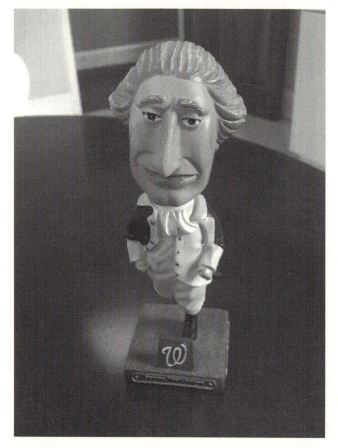

The culprit.

too aligned. The Nats had the game exactly where they wanted it. And that meant – obviously, to me at least– that they were going to lose.

I remembered Daniel Descalso in 2012. I remembered Drew Storen and the 18th inning loss to the Giants in 2014. I remembered Game 5 in 2016. I knew – I knew – that Tantalus was about to strike again.

Obviously, I never imagined the actual details of the disaster that then transpired. Who could? Mad Max, Cy Young winner, rolling single, single, double, intentional walk, wild pitch, error, catchers' interference, and hit by pitch? *All with two outs?* And throw in, for added misery, a blown umpire's call that would have ended the inning with no runs scored? If you don't believe in the Curse of the Nationals after that, you never will.

But now at least we can rest in the knowledge that none of it was Max's fault. It was George Washington's. We traced the curse back, from the Nationals to the Expos, to Steve Rogers and Blue Monday: the same exact disaster as Max in Game 5 against the Cubs.

We followed the trail further back to the 250-year-old French-English conflict in Quebec that led to Bill 101. We examined how the French-only provisions of that bill destroyed Montreal's reign as the financial center of Canada, leading directly to the insolvency of Montreal's baseball team, and thus creating the conditions that required the transfer of the franchise to the capital of the United States.

We continued to delve into the cause of that simmering French-English conflict, the French and Indian War. At last we learned how that war started. The man whose name the former Expos now wear on their chest allowed the butchery and dismemberment of a surrendering French officer named Jumonville.

Thus, the Curse.

While we've discussed the possible answers to remove Jumonville's curse, it remains for others to see it done. But let us remember, that when the Washington Nationals fail to go to the World Series in 2019, they will set a new major league record. They will have spent fifty-one seasons, since their founding in Montreal in 1969, without ever winning a pennant. It is a milestone of abject failure unequaled in the game. No other team in baseball has ever failed to win a pennant in the first five decades of their existence: not the Red Sox, not the Cubs, not the White Sox, nor the Indians. And until Jumonville's ghost is banished from Nationals Park, it seems likely that the Nationals will continue to extend that unhappy record, year after year.

The Red Sox beat their curse, and the Cubs did as well. There is hope perhaps for the Washington Nationals.

THE END.

AFTERWORD

IN ALL GOOD MURDER MYSTERIES, it's important to keep the identity of the killer a secret for other potential readers. I would ask that you not spoil the hunt for others, and keep the identity of the Nats' killer to yourself. Shhhhh --- mum's the word.

There are at least four different eyewitness accounts of what went on at Jumonville Glen, in addition to Washington's brief journal entry. (They include that of a French soldier named Monceau who escaped the massacre entirely and marched back to Fort Duquesne barefoot.) The witnesses' recollections differ fairly significantly on details such as who shot first, and exactly how Jumonville was martyred. For those interested, Fred Anderson's scholarly *Crucible of War* is not only a fantastic history of the French and Indian War, but does an especially excellent job of resolving the conflicting testimony about the events of Jumonville Glen.

For those interested in learning more about the Nationals when they were the Expos, the best account I've found is *Up, Up, and Away* by Jonah Keri. It's a detailed retelling of the team's prior life in Montreal, from start to finish, written with the true affection of a lifelong fan of the Expos.

This book was written without the express written consent, and not even the implied oral consent, of the Washington Nationals or Major League Baseball.

I must render thanks to all those who assisted me in this book. Mark McCaslin let me sit in his restaurant for hours and eat up his wifi while I drank endless cups of coffee and wrote. Steve Chernow and Keith Ausbrook served as initial reviewers. They helped me determine if I was on the right path; their encouragement and insights, from start to finish, were greatly appreciated. Brian McLaughlin and Alex Remington added a second level of review. Their valuable perspectives, Brian as a rabid, present-at-the-creation fan of the Nationals, and Alex as a longtime (published) historian of the emerald chessboard, also made the book better. Contributions of all four of these gentlemen found their way into the pages.

It is always great to relearn that your children have talent. My daughter Grace provided most of the photographs herein (wangling a trip to Montreal out of the process). She also provided editing suggestions, winnowing out some inapt phrases. My son Alex provided invaluable suggestions throughout the process and thankless proofreading and editing of the whole opus. He's a darn good editor, as it turns out. The ritual sacrifice of Screech came from his devious mind.

Finally, I owe particular thanks to two major contributors. First, Rich Lerner, a longtime friend, former Jeopardy champion, and walking Baseball Encyclopedia, saved me from several embarrassing errors, and provided valuable suggestions all throughout the book. Second, Professor Andrew Murr took time out from teaching college sophomores how to write to teach me how to write. His professional editing skills, honed by decades as a journalist, greatly improved sentences, paragraphs, and chapters. Whatever its residual flaws, this book is much better due to their red pens. Any remaining mistakes, factual or syntactic, are mine, not theirs.

Two losses occurred during the writing of this book. We lost Rusty Staub, *Le Grand Orange* himself, just before Opening Day 2018. Rusty was a true gentleman and a boyhood hero of mine. He was easy to root for. I had hoped to interview him for this book, and grieved at his death. I hope he does make it into the Hall someday.

My college teammate and roommate, Brian Laporte, succumbed to leukemia just before Opening Day 2019. Brian was a baseball nut, and, though raised in Hawaii, a lifelong fanatical supporter of the Red Sox, and thus quite familiar with sports curses. He was also an early reviewer of the book, and although he didn't get to see it in final form, I will always treasure the praise he lavished on it. I will miss him.

Made in the USA
Columbia, SC
14 February 2025